TRANSFORMING SCHOOLS

TRANSFORMING SCHOOLS

A Trauma-Informed Approach to Teaching, Learning, and Healing

MARCIA RANGLIN-VASSELL

CREATED IN PARTNERSHIP WITH THE
**LA GONDOLA PROVIDENCE
COMMUNITY FOUNDATION**

WORLDCHANGERS
M E D I A

Paperback ISBN: 978-1-955811-69-9
E-book ISBN: 978-1-955811-70-5
LCCN: 2024905100

First paperback edition: May 2024

Author photo: xxx
Cover artwork: Terrence Vassell
Cover design, layout, and typesetting: Bryna Haynes
Editors: Audra Figgins, Paul Baillie-Lane

Published by WorldChangers Media
PO Box 83, Foster, RI 02825
www.WorldChangers.Media

MY HOPE FOR YOU

I hope you get ...
to walk
run
dance
swim
I hope you get ...
to ride a bike
fly a kite
I hope you get ...
to smile
laugh
giggle
I hope you get ...
to breathe
poke fun at yourself
feel silly
make mistakes
learn from them
I hope you get ...
to smell the coffee
roses
chase pretty painted butterflies
I hope you get ...
to be you

CONTENTS

FOREWORD

BY DARLENE ALLEN, MS

WHEN MARCIA TOLD ME she was writing a book on how trauma shows up in students and how teachers and others can help to mitigate the impact, I was thrilled. I am so honored and truly humbled to write this foreword.

Children are not broken, and they should never be treated as such. Unfortunately, far too many children who have been exposed to traumatic events and display various challenging behaviors are misunderstood. Because many child-serving professionals lack a trauma-informed lens, these children are often not treated or supported in a way that would help promote healing, learning, and positive development. *Transforming Schools: A Trauma-Informed Approach to Teaching, Learning, and Healing* will help to change that. By sharing research, lessons learned from educators in the field, and Marcia's own personal and professional experiences, this book will prove to be a valuable resource for all who want to make a difference in the lives of children.

For almost four decades, I have worked in the child welfare field. It is through meeting so many children and youths who have suffered from abuse and neglect, and experienced profound grief and loss, that I became committed to helping children heal from trauma.

I met Marcia when she was first elected to the Rhode Island House of Representatives. I remember our first meeting. We met at a local bakery in Providence. I was late. I really hate being late, particularly for a first meeting. I felt horrible, but Marcia was so warm and forgiving. We spent an hour talking with each other about all sorts of things. By the end of our meeting, it felt like we had known each other forever. We really connected on the need to advocate for state-level policies that lift up and support children. We discussed senseless gun-related tragedies concerning children from our city and talked about the number of youths we knew who were hungry and homeless. We also shared with each other that we both knew far too many young people who had aged out of foster care. We were saddened by so much suffering. From that time on, we were both determined to stay connected, support each other, and work tirelessly to make a difference in the lives of Rhode Island children, youth, and families.

Throughout the years I have known Marcia, I have known her to be an intelligent, compassionate, and fierce advocate for children. Marcia spends her days in the classroom making a difference in the lives of so many Providence children, and her afternoons and evenings fighting for the rights of all of Rhode Island's children. As a former legislator, she was always strong, consistent, and unwavering in her fight for a more just and equitable world. Marcia is committed to standing up and speaking out for children, even when others dismiss her. I am so appreciative of her dedication to advocating for the rights of children.

Over the years, Marcia and I have often met with each other and diverse groups of community members to talk about ways we can address trauma. We have discussed many ideas and created different strategies to embed trauma knowledge into our schools, communities, and other child-serving systems. Prior to COVID-19, we were gaining great momentum, but the pandemic put a sudden halt to our plans for robust community engagement.

By 2021, stories about the impact of trauma and toxic stress on children were flooding the media. The issue is now in the public square, and there is no denying its impact. Legislators were also more informed and became increasingly interested in strategies to help children succeed. In 2022, we doubled down and became laser-focused on re-engaging community members and child advocates to get a bill passed that would create trauma-informed schools across Rhode Island. Our team met regularly throughout the legislative session and spoke almost daily for months. There were days I lifted Marcia up, and days she lifted me up. Marcia worked diligently and collaboratively to successfully get the Trauma-Informed Schools Act bill passed and signed into Rhode Island's law. I have so much respect, love, and admiration for Marcia. She is the real deal.

In addition to Marcia's strengths as a legislator and policy-maker, she is an excellent writer and storyteller. She is a published poet, educator, helper, listener, and leader. Marcia has a wealth of knowledge and has always been generous to those of us who are fortunate to know her. She lives and breathes equity, justice, and opportunity. She knows trauma on a personal level and, as an educator in an urban public-school setting, has witnessed the impact of trauma on so many of the children she serves.

While children are not broken, many systems are. So many educators are struggling with mental health and behavioral issues in students who need help. Many have spoken about feeling overwhelmed, unsupported, and not as effective as they would like to be. This book will be an invaluable resource to these educators and other childcare professionals. It offers a better understanding of the impact of toxic stress and trauma on the developing child as well as strategies to help you, the reader, truly see kids who are struggling and work with them more effectively. This book will help you to imagine schools as a place of learning, nurturing, healing, and support where all children can thrive.

Darlene Allen, MS, *is the CEO of a non-profit organization that serves foster and adopted children, youth, and families. She has dedicated over four decades to caring for our most vulnerable children.*

FOREWORD

BY MELISSA JENKINS MANGILI, PHD

WHEN I BEGAN MY research career examining the neuropsychology of traumatic stress in the 1990s, most of what we knew about the brain's response to traumatic events came from research on military veterans. The impact of war had been further studied with each respective generation of returned soldiers, so we'd learned that cognitive changes and psychological symptoms were common aftereffects of war. We were only beginning to understand that other traumatic events also impact neuropsychology. Trauma including rape, domestic violence, child abuse and neglect, gun violence, and other life and death situations were all events that occurred with much higher frequency than exposure to war.

In the past three decades, we have learned that traumatic events not only shape our short-term psychology and cognition, but that traumatic stress can even alter the structure of our brain. For example, corticosteroids are one mediator of the fight-or-flight response that seem preferentially neurotoxic to the hippocampus, which plays a key role in memory. Indeed, there are demonstrable changes to attention and memory functioning across trauma groups, showing that it's not the type of trauma *per se*, but our reaction to it that may most affect how our brains will respond and adapt over time to traumatic experiences. Trauma-induced changes to the brain can result in varying degrees of cognitive dysfunction and emotional dysregulation, including impaired attention and memory, symptoms of depression or anxiety expressed in a multitude of ways, impaired social skills, sleep disturbance, or difficulty with behavioral self-control.

Have you heard the phrase "problem child?" In some cases, this means "traumatized child." In other cases, the child may not show behavioral symptoms, but may not fulfill their academic potential. They may withdraw socially or have difficulty relating to peers or adults. In academic settings, we often do not know why a child is behaving as they are. We have little chance outside of the school setting to understand or to impact their experience. This makes it all the more important to consider the conditions in which our children live and adapt the culture of our educational system accordingly. The goal is not to turn school personnel into doctors, but to create a broad, inclusive culture that can better anticipate and meet the needs of students coming to schools with traumatic histories.

Nobody is better aware of the importance of trauma-informed school systems than Marcia Ranglin-Vassell. She has worked on the front lines of schools from Bull Bay, Jamaica, to Providence, Rhode Island, teaching thousands of students over a four-decade teaching career across cultures and eras, which shaped her understanding of the critical universal elements for student success. In addition to her extensive background in Special Education and Trauma-Informed School Training, she was responsible for the formation and implementation of a Study Commission to advise the development of school programs incorporating evidence-based practices to better respond to the need for trauma-informed educational programming. Her vast experience and passionate advocacy as a teacher also formed the basis for her community activism, leading her to a position as an elected representative in the Rhode Island legislature.

Throughout her tenure, Marcia taught state officials about schools, conveying the needs of her students, fellow teachers, and all school personnel. Her views are not hers alone; they have been shaped, to a great extent, by her fellow educators, administrators, constituents, advisors, and perhaps most importantly, by the thousands of students who passed through her classroom over the years. Across eras, across cultures, and across continents, the universality of the experience of trauma and its various expressions within the educational system became clear.

Ever the teacher, she taught Rhode Island the importance of trauma-informed education, and the critical steps for the successful evolution of our educational system. She now hopes to share these insights more broadly. As much as it will educate our heads, this book will speak to the hearts of those who care about children. Understanding, after all, depends on creating an atmosphere for self-exploration, creative interaction with new ideas, and engagement. These pages engender that atmosphere, and the beginning of the process that can transform our schools—through each of us—with a culture of trauma-informed teaching, behavioral adaptation, and inclusive understanding.

Teacher, activist, former lawmaker, author, expert advisor, parent, and now architect of a plan for transformative change in our collective mindset about what it means to educate, Marcia knows that you can't teach a student you can't reach. Bridging communication gaps is not only about language or ideology, it's also about cultural relevance; creating environments that facilitate acceptance, growth, and self-expression; and fostering emotional development as a conduit for intellectual development.

Transforming Schools: A Trauma-Informed Approach to Teaching, Learning, and Healing is a blueprint designed to transform our thinking about trauma and facilitate children's development in a culture where trauma is much too common.

Dr. Melissa Jenkins Mangili *is a neuropsychologist and the director at Brainworks. She is an internationally recognized expert on the effects of PTSD on cognitive functioning.*

INTRODUCTION

I WAS A POOR GIRL growing up in poverty, with the odds of succeeding stacked against me. Who could have thought that decades later my improbable journey would take me from the ghettos of Kingston, Jamaica, to become a powerful and transformative voice in the Rhode Island House of Representatives? I didn't go to these influential chambers alone. I brought with me the resolute voices and the stories of children just like me, whose lives have been upended by childhood trauma.

Besides time, the only major thing that separates my students and me is the geographic boundaries—I grew up in Jamaica, where both of my parents were born. My dad, Eric Ranglin, would tell my siblings and I the story of him running away as a young lad because he was suffering from physical abuse at his home in the Jamaican countryside. He made his way to Kingston, the capital and largest city on the island. Dad never had the opportunity to read or write, but he was educated in other ways and was very street savvy. My mom, Mavis, was forced out of school in the sixth grade to earn money, which she did by washing clothes for rich people in Town, which is what the locals call Kingston. As one of the oldest siblings in her family, she also had to help take care of her younger brothers and sisters. Mom never had the opportunity to go back to school to complete her education. She would wash clothes for the remainder of her life, even after she emigrated to the United States.

My parents met and had nine children, and they were both extremely dedicated to us. Because of the difficult circumstances of their own lives, it was important for them to raise a successful and loving family. I'm the middle child of nine. I was born on a rainy and gloomy Saturday morning in May, 1960. I was a quintessential middle child that no one seemed to remember. The one that became the caregiver, the nurturer. It makes sense that I wanted to be a teacher and spend my life helping others!

I was born in Eleven Miles, Bull Bay, an area on the southeast coast of Jamaica that got its name for being eleven miles from the bustling capital city of Kingston. My entire community was poor, and hardly any person I knew had a professional job. Mostly, everyone did menial work and tried their best to get by on almost nothing. Only a lucky few escaped the area to get a job in Town. For example, my aunt Violet was one of the lucky ones to get domestic work in Harbour View, a place where the well-to-do mostly lived.

We lived in government-provided housing. Decades later, I called up my older sister, Pearline, and asked her if we lived in a project. The term "project" wasn't used to name government housing at the time, but having lived in the US for thirty-plus years now, I can see the similarities. The "project" we lived in was called Cambridge Farm Housing Scheme, but we all just called it "The Scheme." It consisted of twenty-six two-room board houses with no inside plumbing, running water, or public transportation to get us from one place to another. We had no mail carriers, so we had to walk a mile away to collect letters. If someone died in another parish, there was the occasional telegram that Bredda Man, the mailman, hurriedly brought announcing the death of loved ones. Later, as a teen, I would regularly take the mile walk in the broiling sun, saying I wanted to get a letter but secretly hoping to see my teenage crush, Michael.

Once in a blue moon, USAID would bring free food for us, and all the families would form a ridiculously long line at Brother Will's shop to collect the food. We waited in line for hours to get a fraction of what we needed, but my mom was always grateful for the rice, flour, and salt fish. She knew how to stretch it to make it last for a long time and feed her nine children. That was my mom; she was a genius at making things work. My father, although he couldn't read and write—he would scrawl a crooked X when he had to sign important papers—also made things work. He and my mother were rich in dreams, and they wanted more for their children. They were staunch advocates of education, knowing that faith and education was the only way to unlock the shackles of poverty. Therefore, in 1963, and right smack in the front yard of our humble abode, dubbed Lot 23, Dad opened a Basic School (Pre-K), which extended from the two-room house I shared with my parents and siblings. It was there that the seed for learning was planted. Simultaneously, Dad started the New Testament Church of God alongside a couple of other people who were committed to bringing the word of God to hungry souls: Brother and Sister Fisher, Deacon Holding, and Evangelist Jackson. Since Sister Fisher could read and write, she became the teacher at the Basic School. Soon, Lot 23 was the most popular spot in the area. Folks had a school to send their kids to during the day and a place to worship at night.

Though poor, my life was pretty routine. Mostly, I remember attending school by day and church by night, and playing ring games with my siblings and other neighborhood children to break the monotony. I still have a scar above my left eye from Georgie rolling me in a truck tire so fast I fell out and hit the ground. I guess that was a foreshadowing of the number of rises and falls I would encounter in my adult life. The community allowed a space for kids to play together while men worked together in the fields and while their wives sat and talked together. Those were my best days growing up in Eleven Miles, playing ring games while the men played dominoes sitting on the shop "Paza," which is what the locals called the storefront.

Sixty years later, I now see that Dad was quite the visionary. With all the bad and evil acts in our neighborhood, the church that Dad started remains a place of refuge and prayer. His church and Basic School set up the futures of his children, and I'm happy to report that they are still educating children and bringing lost souls to Jesus Christ. This school was, and is, very important because life in Bull Bay is characterized by visceral hardship, pain, and trauma. Successive generations have experienced the same fate under successive governments who didn't value their citizens as human beings. Notwithstanding all the trauma and toxicity, we endured, we valued each other, loved each other, looked out for each other.

It was in these humble beginnings that I developed the lifelong love for reading and writing and a true appreciation for education. While growing up, no other person except for Ellen, one of my distant cousins, went to college. After college, Ellen came back to the district and taught at my primary school. In fact, she was my science and Spanish teacher. My sister, Val, would follow Ellen years later to attend high school and finish college. Val was the first person in my immediate family to attend college. Lucky to have had such a positive role model, I would soon follow in her footsteps.

I was also lucky to have a few teachers who understood the importance of creating meaningful and safe spaces in my school. I remember Ms. Simpson, a friendly, welcoming teacher. She did a nice job connecting to her students, including me. She was a bright-eyed, always smartly dressed, and absolutely stunning fifth-grade teacher—a goddess. She spoke proper English, which I tried to emulate to no avail. I was enamored! I never quite understood why she took a liking to me, but she did. Ms. Simpson would share her lunch with me, and at the end of the school week, she would sometimes take me home with her for the weekend. Her house was cradled deep in western St. Thomas, a humble home she shared with her mom, dad, brothers, and sisters. It was a much safer area of the parish than the violence-prone area where I lived. My parents were happy to know I was safe, and probably glad to have one less mouth to feed! I loved spending those extra days with Ms. Simpson. I didn't have clothes to take, so I'd spend the weekend in her dresses that were much too big for a skinny little girl like me. I didn't care. Being at her house also meant I wouldn't go to bed hungry or have to hide under the bed listening to a barrage of gunshots. Ms. Simpson was a true hero, and another one of my influences in becoming a teacher. I wanted to be able to give back to kids just like she did for me. I will forever be paying back their generosity through the work I do now. I'm here today because of teachers who loved and cared for me, and poured into me like I was their own.

While the community helped me grow and survive in the midst of poverty, it was certainly not without trauma. Over the years, I held a lot of shame about not being able to afford basic necessities. I still remember walking to school without shoes and a book bag, so I'd tuck my books into my blouse to protect them from the rain. There were times I had to use the pages of the local newspaper, the *Jamaica Daily Gleaner*, as sanitary napkins because I didn't have any. I'm sure my older sisters would have helped me, but I was so either too ashamed, too prideful, or too scared to ask for what I needed. This memory has never left me. The truth is that no child should ever experience the shame and guilt of having their period. Period.

There were times I pretended to be sick the night before a school concert or other activity where we'd have to wear casual clothes and not our school uniforms. I feared being one of the only girls in my class to show up wearing that ridiculous blue tunic and white blouse because I didn't have any other nice clothes. I didn't want to face the ridicule of other students. No child should ever have to miss out on learning because of a lack of access to necessities, including clean clothes or sanitary napkins. It's the very reason I began a hygiene closet in a school that I taught at, partnering with like-minded individuals to ensure that kids had access to hygiene products, clean items of clothing, and emergency food. The basic necessities help to uphold the dignity of all children.

There were also days that I couldn't attend school because my parents didn't have the money for us to buy school lunches. Ms. Tanisha, my mother's friend, was a short, heavy-set woman who sold lunches at her home, and often Mom would have us ask her to give us lunches "to trust," meaning we'd pay later. When she was in a good mood, Ms. Tanisha would give us lunches on credit, but when she wasn't, she would yell at us and chase us away. The trauma memory of a growling stomach and being chased away just for trying to get a fifteen-cent bottle of Kool-Aid drink and fried fritters was also the impetus for me years later in the General Assembly, when I worked to ensure that Rhode Island ended lunch shaming in all public schools. That work continues, even though I'm no longer an elected official.

As much as I loved school, I hated when Mom would show up for meetings. She would come with a head tie that only really poor women wore and her favorite slippers, which she'd made from shoes too worn, too old, and too raggedy to be shoes anymore. I remember hiding so she didn't see me. There was no way in hell I was going to let the other kids know that poor-looking woman was my mother! I see this same attitude in my students today. Some are ashamed of their parents, and it's that shame that poor children carry deep in their souls.

There's also shame and trauma that occurs for those that try to move beyond poverty. While at school, I did all my work to get good grades, but I was bullied. This is because many students in poverty don't see education as a way out, and therefore, when a student tries in school, it's not always supported and valued by their peers. For example, one of the worst bullies was a girl in my class named Diana. She would sit behind me in class and pull my hair. As if that wasn't enough, she even put a sharp pencil under my bottom every time I stood up to answer a question, hoping I would sit on it. I thought she bullied me simply because I was smart and did my work. I was right. There was absolutely no other reason.

One Friday, under my cousin Nee Nee's guinep tree, the bullying finally came crashing to a halt. I was fed up with Diana's constant harassment and bullying, so instead of deflecting or running away, I confronted her and we got into a physical fight. I won, and she never bullied me again. Later, I realized that Diana's bullying was just a manifestation of what she was seeing at home. Her dad was a meek man who was constantly bullied by her mom, who was addicted to alcohol. It wasn't about me at all. I was just a good target.

I wish I could tell Diana how sorry I am that I fought her, although she's since passed away. At the time, fighting back felt like my only option. My school didn't have a policy about bullying. My parents were too busy worrying about how to get food on the table, and I didn't want to add something else to their plate, so I didn't tell them. But I wish that someone had seen that I was being bullied, and that both of us needed help. Creating safe spaces for all children is paramount to improving student outcomes as well as safety for staff.

Often concealed beneath violent outbursts, aggressive tendencies, or disruptive behaviors lies a darker truth. These behaviors, though seemingly chaotic and bewildering, are simply the manifestation of trauma. If teachers make building robust and healthy relationships with their students a priority, children will be more open to sharing what's going on in their lives and asking for support. This is absolutely necessary in communities where poverty is not the only issue that traumatizes children.

Innocence Lost

Prior to the 1970s, when there was an emergence of political violence from the feuding rival members of the Jamaica Labour Party and the People's National Party, we lived peacefully. We could go to our beds without the fear of gunshots bellowing at nights, and without the fear of waking to find friends or loved ones killed. Kids could play cricket in the streets. And there was no fear of walking to the post office to collect letters. All that changed when my crush's eleven-year-old brother, Tom, was shot and killed. Now, forty-plus years later, unemployment, gun violence, and tragedy remain rooted around "The Scheme" and the place I still call home.

It wasn't that my mom and dad didn't do everything to protect us. They did. In fact, in his desire to shield us, Dad even erected a twelve-foot zinc fence around our house. But even with a physical fence, we couldn't escape the trauma that surrounded us; that lived with us day in and day out, waiting for us beyond the zinc fence.

I was fourteen when my innocence was taken. My granduncle, Uncle Newton, a special constable and well-read man, was tragically shot and killed in his sleep, not by strangers but obviously by people he knew. Allegedly, he was killed by young people who might have wanted his licensed firearm to commit acts of violence. The morning of that day is seared in my memory because Ted,

Kevon, and Thompson, three neighborhood boys who we all knew and went to school with, were also shot and killed. The sudden and violent deaths of these four people shook me to my core, but it was only the beginning. I would soon bear witness to a string of gun violence homicides against family, friends, classmates, neighbors, and random strangers. Sad to say, these preventable deaths were rooted in structural poverty.

In fact, I can tell you all the names of the people who were shot and killed when I was growing up. Often the trauma witnessed by a child is something they continue to experience over and over throughout their lives. Decades later, I'm now living in a country I had only dreamed about as a child, yet the epidemic of gun violence exists here, too. According to the Centers for Disease Control and Prevention, gun-related deaths are the leading cause of deaths among children and teens. Sadly, this continues unabated. This is preventable violence that we must work to end, and at the same time to help children who have tragically been exposed to heal and carry on.

Trying to escape the violence that surrounded me, at the age of eighteen I decided that I wanted to "get the hell out of Bull Bay." I opted first to go to Bethlehem's Teacher's College, a quiet, peaceful place far away in the countryside of Jamaica. After the first year on campus, I didn't return and headed back home to Bull Bay. After a year of uncertainty, I was lucky to be invited to participate in a one-year community service program with the Social Development Commission, a social services and advocacy organization located in downtown Kingston, where participants earned a small stipend while helping the community. Unfortunately, violence found me again when, one Friday, my Area 3 supervisor told me that my cousin, Dennis, had been shot and killed. It didn't matter where I was in Jamaica; in a country of rampant political upheaval and readily available firearms, tragedy and trauma followed me. After completing the one year of service, I was accepted to St. Joseph's Teacher's College in Kingston, a Franciscan Order Catholic women's college.

Unfortunately, in 1982, and after less than a month in college, Dad suddenly passed away from septic shock. I was twenty-two. My family's daily struggle to stay afloat intensified. After a tough four years, I graduated with a Diploma in Elementary Education, which was equivalent to a Bachelor's here in the US. Meanwhile, Mom did her best to keep it together by selling fruits in the neighborhood. We began to pin all of our hopes on getting out of Jamaica. My mom's sister, Auntie Violet, lived in Providence, Rhode Island, and my mom yearned to join her there and make a better life. Mom was on the verge of giving up coming to the US when a big brown envelope from the American Embassy located in Kingston arrived. It was sent directly from the US Citizenship and Immigration Services. It was an invitation for her to travel to Kingston to do a physical. In order to travel to the US back then, you had to take a physical, which included a HIV test. Mom decided to take three of my siblings along for the test. They passed! Mom didn't have much money at the time, so when she was ready to join Auntie Violet, she was only able to take my youngest sister, Lisa, with her. Four years later in 1990, my own brown envelope arrived. I almost jumped out of my clothes. Finally, I hoped, I would escape the poverty, violence, trauma, and everything in between!

Gleefully, I landed at JFK International Airport on a summer evening in June 1990. My heart skipped with joy thinking that I had left the violence and homicides behind. Finally, I could divorce myself from the trauma that had become so much a part of my life. I was wrong. Unbeknownst to me, it found its way into my suitcase and followed me all the way to Prairie Avenue in Providence, Rhode Island.

First, I realized that the United States doesn't easily open its arms to immigrants. Like many individuals who emigrate to the US with college degrees, I was unable to get a job in my chosen career field of teaching. My four-year degree was not acknowledged by the school district I applied to. Armed with determination and a tenacious attitude, I didn't let the disappointment break my spirit. As the old song we sang in church reminded me, it was "too far to turn back now." I searched relentlessly every day, knocking on doors that displayed an "Employment Wanted" sign. I was hungry for a job. After a few years of not teaching, I finally secured a teaching job at the Urban League of Rhode Island while simultaneously attending Rhode Island College. The job at the Urban League, a social services agency contracted to provide continuing education for students receiving out-of-school suspension for up to forty-five days, was different from what I had been accustomed to at John Mills All Age School in Kingston. Whereas my school in Kingston educated students with supportive communities that promoted their futures, many of the students at the Urban League had been adjudicated, and many saw the education system as having failed them. Changing their mindset was difficult, but I was determined to make it work for those children who deserved so much more than they had received.

Then the unthinkable happened. I lost one of my students, Tyson, to gun violence. Just like losing my granduncle had been the beginning of a string of unbearable losses, this child's tragic death ushered in a string of homicides that would also hit close to my heart. This was the moment I realized that many of my students were just like me, despite our differing backgrounds. I had a rude awakening: being in America didn't solve all my problems, and many children were experiencing the same kinds of trauma I was exposed to as a child. There was nothing different except the location.

It's easy to lose hope when all that you see around you is hopelessness, to grow tired and weary when everyone around you is traumatized. It's easy to turn on the world in anger, thinking that the world turned on you and hasn't given you even one second of grace. But I couldn't. Each day, I saw the faces of my students, the issues they were still facing, the trauma they were still carrying around. I knew I had to be part of making change happen, making their classrooms and their worlds into better and more supportive places.

For some unknown reason, the universe gives me boys! I either gave birth to boys, was gifted with grandsons, or had them on my class roster. Either way, I cannot escape boys.

This is what I thought as I looked at the seven high school aged boys whose special education class I had randomly been assigned to teach. This was one of my very first teaching gigs with the public school system. Although certified in English and Special Education, this class was Self-Contained, which meant I was expected to teach every single subject, including mathematics. "I can't do math," I often joked, adding, "I don't want math in my life at all." But seriously, I'm not going to say that I'm a math genius—but for the students in my class, I devoted lots of out-of-school practice to be able to teach it.

I also had to devote a lot of emotional energy to support an obviously marginalized group of young men. This is because the school district leaders had chosen to relegate the special education classroom to a dingy basement space—something that I've seen come up many times since that first experience. Too often it seems as though we isolate and "other" children who have had significant challenges or experienced trauma in their young lives. To single kids out and essentially remove them from the larger school community is an injustice in and of itself. But there I was with my assistant, Ms. Juana, and the seven boys who kept us on our toes. We shared the same dingy, windowless room all day.

I'll always remember Kyle, a biracial boy with an afro that was perfectly set. It was like his afro was placed on his head at birth. He was a beautiful child with a disarming smile. He'd flash that smile when he wanted to, especially if he thought it could work in his favor, such as when he was angling for an "A". Kyle was a different kind of kid! He was charmingly beautiful, helpful, and loving when he wanted to be, accepting my compliments and complimenting me back with gusto. At other times, he wasn't in control of his emotions and would impulsively toss chairs, cursing at everyone in sight. When Kyle decided to focus with the rest of the class, I was humbled—or, perhaps more accurately, humiliated—by his sheer math sense and ability to grasp concepts across every single content area. He could do the work, but mostly he refused to.

Instead, he spent the days finding a target to pick on and bully. He got mad at me when I intervened to ensure that the classroom remained safe for all. Kyle pushed back on everything I said. He poked fun at me and made me feel like I had zero idea what I was doing. He pushed my buttons every day and was severely disruptive, yelling and using profanity. I called the principal many times to come to the classroom, and soon, he gave me an ultimatum.

"Suspend him, Mrs. Ranglin-Vassell, or I will not be coming back to the basement."

Suspending a child who didn't necessarily like school in the first place wasn't an option for me. It didn't make sense. It didn't take into consideration Kyle's struggles in his home life—something that followed him and surely haunted him each day at school. And if I suspended him, where was he supposed to go? In the streets to be shot and killed or assaulted? Who would take care of him? I didn't know Kyle's mom, and he'd told me when we first met that his mom was strung out on drugs. After that, he didn't talk much about her. Instead, he spoke highly and lovingly of his sister, Kinte. Though barely older than he was, she was his legal guardian. She came in for meetings when he got in trouble and always seemed so upset, saying, "Here he goes again." I felt bad every time I had to call Kinte, but there was no one else on his contact list. She was trying to build her own life while being pulled in so many directions, and while his sister loved him dearly, she wouldn't be able to stay home with him all day during a suspension. I put that idea aside, deciding not to inform anyone about the issues going on in the basement room. I'd figure something else out. Something that would help Kyle.

After that last visit from the principal, I decided it didn't matter what Kyle did. As long as he didn't hurt himself or others, it was fine. If he didn't want to participate, that was okay too. I considered it a win if he did his own thing quietly without disrupting the rest of the class. He was at school, safe, and that's all I could ask for. For the most part, I left Kyle alone, inconspicuously checking in on him to make sure he was on task. He was. Before long, he began participating, turning in completed assignments and joining in with classroom activities. For some kids, they just need to be left alone for a bit and eventually they will come around. I soon gave him the job of passing out papers and collecting them at the end of class. Before long, I saw smiles bursting out on his beautiful face. My heart smiled.

Our school days were atypical. I learned that to reach my boys, I couldn't just teach the content. In fact, I found it useful to spend time on relationship building by talking to my students and facilitating the students in talking to each other, learning about one another, and strengthening bonds of friendship. These skills are important in teaching and learning. None takes precedence over the others. Great teachers make time for these "softer" skills. Later, I would learn that this is social-emotional instruction and, even later still, I would see how the combination of the two teaching styles would have an impact on students like Kyle.

Seven years later, when I contracted for the renovation of my bathroom at home, I was sitting at my kitchen table having breakfast when two men walked in, accompanied by my husband, Van. Their presence immediately struck me. One was about six foot three and a big guy, which contrasted greatly with his four-foot companion. "Good morning," came their roaring voices, almost like a chorus, as though they had rehearsed the line several times before.

"Good morning," I managed to say between biting into my veggie omelet. One of the voices sounded familiar. It was a bit huskier and coarser than I remembered, but the tone, joy, and inflections were still there! I know that face, I thought to myself as my husband showed the men down the hall to the bathroom. I quickly dismissed the thought and continued eating.

I headed off to work, only to get a call soon after from my husband. Speaking in his Jamaican patois (the dialect that Jamaicans use when they're not in formal settings: a derivative of English, Spanish, and African languages spoken by the settlers or the colonizers on the island), "Di young man ask if mi wife is ah teacha?" In that moment, I knew. That big guy had been Kyle, now working for a reputable construction company. He was in my house making my bathroom beautiful. I felt a huge rush of pride, knowing he might have overcome some of the trauma he'd experienced in childhood. The thought energized me all day and encouraged my work with my students. All through the school day I kept seeing Kyle's face in all of their faces. They would do marvelous things with their lives in the future, and I'd be there to witness it.

Later that evening, I reentered our tiny kitchen and Kyle was there with a huge smile on his face. Without saying any words, he hugged me. Here stood Kyle in my home, many years after sitting in the basement classroom that I'd tried to make into a home for all my students. He was now a young man, a young father, and as beautiful as when I first met him—minus the perfect afro. I chuckled to myself because in place of his perfectly adorned afro, he now had a neat haircut with a sprinkling of gray peeking out.

"I knew you could do it, Kyle! I knew you could," I told him. As he towered over me, I hugged him, much like I had hugged the small boy years ago. I couldn't stop the tears of joy. We hugged each other, not wanting to let go, but eventually, he needed to get back to ripping out the bathtub.

Seeing Kyle again made me realize that we can't give up on kids, especially those who are disruptive or struggling in class. We've got to look beyond what our eyes can literally see. Our kids live traumatic lives, but with love, patience, understanding, and support, they will thrive and become productive members of our community. I know this from experience. During my time as a student and in my decades as an educator, I've heard folks who should be supporting kids instead denigrate them, writing them off as "bad eggs" who will amount to nothing. While I understand and appreciate the difficulties of teaching, particularly in urban schools, no one should be giving up on children. The children who may be struggling the most are the ones who need more adults in their lives who care about them and can offer stability and love.

Teaching is a difficult job. That's an undeniable fact. While all teachers have their own unique reason for wanting to teach, their own WHY, one thing is certainly true: children are the future. Therefore, it's necessary to give them the best possible chance of success in life. Of course, this isn't as straightforward a goal as it seems. It takes hard work, grit, and stubborn determination to help kids, especially those who experience trauma, toxic stress, and chronic stress—topics we'll discuss in Part One of this book.

The foundation of *Transforming Schools: A Trauma-Informed Approach to Teaching, Learning, and Healing* is built on the premise that children are not irrevocably damaged; they are beautiful, whole, and resilient. Given the right level of support in their schools and broader community, kids will be able to heal and thrive. That support cannot be transactional, meaning, "If you do this, you get this." Instead, it must be grounded in love, care, compassion, and empathy. It must come with a deep understanding of how all experiences impact a child's brain architecture, development, and behavior. Children don't need pity; they need love, support, empathy, resources, and healthy relationships with adults who care for them. Kids have dreams and they need caring and compassionate adults around them who believe in those dreams. It takes intentional work to help kids succeed.

The Future of Schooling

So where do things go wrong in the classroom? There are two interrelated questions at play here: why do students display adverse behaviors, and why are these behaviors met with increasingly harsh disciplinary actions, especially in the case of Black children, brown children, children in foster care, and those receiving special education services?

First, students display adverse behaviors because there are very few children whose lives have not been impacted by Adverse childhood experiences (ACEs). Trauma and toxic stress are nothing new. They didn't just pop up out of nowhere. As long as there is systemic racism, structural poverty, gun violence, suicide, hunger, or other adverse childhood experiences, there is and will always be trauma. While I've seen schools do an awesome job responding to the needs of children who experience trauma, I've also witnessed schools where individuals fail miserably in providing care for kids in crisis. This disappoints and saddens me since schools should always be sacred places and safe havens for all students.

Therefore, to answer the second question, the behavior of the students is being met with increasingly harsh actions because school districts are still not fully connecting the dots, even after the pandemic unearthed astounding racial, ethnic, and gender-based disparities. In public schools, policy decisions often rely on testing data, ignoring the human needs of our students. This can be exacerbated by the move to more corporate controlled schools run by CEOs as opposed to principals. While I hesitate to suggest that all schools run by CEOs are not supportive of children, I worry that money is taking precedence over positive student outcomes. There has to be a shift where school leaders intentionally acknowledge the impact of the ACEs on their students' mental health. Then, they must be willing to change their one-sided, data-driven focus to one that embraces a trauma-informed school culture and centers the holistic needs of children as opposed to corporate bosses or a bottom line. If we rely singularly on data-driven production models, many schools will still be very unsafe places that cause further harm to kids.

So, why were trauma-informed educational practices not included in most teacher and administrator education programs, including my own education through graduate school, prior to George Floyd and COVID-19? The answer lies in systems that have "othered," marginalized, or discredited an entire group of kids, many of whom have now become statistics in the prison complex system. Before I go on, let me be clear, this book is not about casting stones or laying blame. It's about acknowledging socio-cultural and oppressive education systems that must change in response to the mental health crisis that kids are experiencing. One of the goals of this book is to help school districts create trauma-informed and trauma-aware schools. In addition, I seek to create an awareness of the impact of adverse childhood experiences: hunger, poverty, classism, colorism, systemic racism, and gun violence on children.

Trauma-informed schools are schools in which all members of the team know how to recognize trauma symptoms, are empowered to make referrals, and can access community resources in a timely manner. Creating trauma-informed schools must be intentional and school-wide, involving any adult whom children interact with on a daily basis. This means everyone rowing their boat in the same direction, and everyone lifting as they are climbing.

The bedrock of a trauma-informed school is creating spaces inside of the classroom, on the field, in the gymnasium, in the cafeteria, and anywhere in a school that are safe, healthy, welcoming, and supportive to all children and their diverse families. When children and families enter the doors of their school, they should see and speak to folks who look like them, speak their language, and identify with their social, cultural, ethnic, or racial background. Representation matters. In order to effect change, we must be willing to have uncomfortable conversations that are meaningful and respectful, and that will move us toward the goal of creating schools where every child is welcomed and valued.

Creating trauma-informed schools cannot be done alone. There must be an all-hands-and-hearts-on-deck approach. For trauma-informed schools to work, there needs to be buy-in from every single staff member. Everyone must be eager to learn about how trauma from children's lived experiences affects not only the developing brain but also impacts teaching. It's a herculean task, and teachers cannot be the only people with this focus. That would be tantamount to herding cats—impossible! Therefore, this applies to school administrators, crossing guards, bus drivers, secretaries, custodians, behavior interventionists, social workers, canteen or cafeteria staff, paraprofessionals, school nurse-teachers, and every other kind of caregiver working with kids. So, in addition to my own voice, this book lifts up the voices of teachers, administrators, coaches, mental health professionals, and other school personnel who support children in the school setting. This book provides good medicine and strategies for folks who value diversity, equity, and inclusion, and who strive to practice compassionate, anti-racist student engagement through trauma-informed care. Creating opportunities for resilience and a place where students can thrive must be our collective focus. This is a lot, but I see the sunshine through the rain; I see the butterfly that will emerge from the cocoon. I'm here to shed light and to help.

What to Expect from this Book

Writing a book of this nature has been heavy on my mind and heart for many years now. *Transforming Schools: A Trauma-Informed Approach to Teaching, Learning, and Healing* provides accessible, concrete, and practical examples of what practitioners can do to create and maintain classrooms where everyone is valued, differences are respected, and multiple opportunities to grow and thrive are provided.

This is not a "How to Fix These Kids" book. The work of becoming trauma-informed is not that simple; it's not a one-size-fits-all. So, rather than telling you what to do, my goal is to provide you with a foundation of understanding to begin or boost your trauma-informed journey. Using a holistic approach to teaching, the goal is predicated on promoting learning that's authentic, academic, and focused on the social and emotional aspects of life. According to the Centers for Disease Control and Prevention, Social-Emotional Learning (SEL) "teaches young people the skills to recognize and manage emotions, set and achieve positive goals, appreciate the perspectives of others, establish and maintain positive relationships, and make responsible decisions." This is vital in a trauma-informed classroom.

In Part One, we'll explore Social-Emotional Learning. This means we'll gain a deeper understanding of what trauma is, what adverse childhood experiences are, and how these experiences affect children's development and behavior. When classroom teachers don't understand what trauma is or how chronic and toxic stress affect students, they can't be expected to teach effectively in a trauma-informed or trauma-aware way.

Part Two focuses on providing a greater explanation of what it means to be "trauma-informed," sharing case studies and anecdotes about what this looks like in practice. I also share my journey as a former elected member of the Rhode Island House of Representatives and the process of getting the Trauma-Informed Schools Act passed and signed into law.

Part Three offers strategies that you can utilize to inform and improve your practice that will not only benefit your students but will also encourage you to teach effectively while avoiding burnout. Teachers don't get half the credit they have earned. In fact, we are often punching bags and get blamed for almost everything that goes wrong in education. Of course, when things go right, everyone and their grannies line up to take the credit. The truth is teachers are first responders. We are in the trenches, supporting children every day. Thank you to the teachers who roll up their sleeves every day to teach children in spite of insurmountable challenges.

As I struggled with the idea of how to write a book of this nature, one that I thought would better equip educators with the knowledge and skill sets to better understand adverse childhood experiences, I tried to conceptualize and understand my own pedagogy and response to teaching kids who struggle with trauma and toxic stress. I decided my perspective didn't go far enough and I wanted to hear from others to get a better understanding of what they saw and how they responded to the needs of the children in their classrooms Therefore, I needed to get input from key stakeholders including teachers, administrators, and paraprofessionals. Thus, throughout the book, I offer stories from my lived experience, as well as those from other teachers, practitioners, and students. Including their voices was key to crafting this book.

Initially, I thought that I would do a community listening tour. Although I would have loved to do the tour, I just didn't have enough time. I was teaching full-time, while also doing my after-school gig as a part-time legislator. This meant full-time responsibilities of responding to my constituents' calls and letters, staying late to testify on bills, introducing new bills, and all of the countless hours of work to research legislation. I was also a full-time mom, wife, grandmother, and caregiver. So instead, I came up with the idea of an informal five-question survey. I reached out to some current and former colleagues personally, and also shared a request for respondents on social media. The number of responses was not overwhelming, but the quality of the responses was both authentic and solid.

The survey questions were:

1). Why did you decide to become a teacher and how long have you been teaching?

2). Where did you first learn about trauma-informed learning, and was it in your teacher education program?

3). How do you respond to children in your school who have traumatic and/or adverse experiences?

4). Do you think that you're adequately prepared to teach or interact with children experiencing trauma? Explain.

5). Describe your idea of a trauma-informed school?

Respondents were teachers as well as social workers, school administrators, and other childcare paraprofessionals. The classroom teachers who participated in the survey had a combined

287 years of classroom instructional experience. They came from different geographic regions of the United States, from suburbia to the urban core, and from different countries, from Laos to Jamaica. Through their responses to the survey questions, I gauged their knowledge of what adverse childhood experiences are, what trauma-informed practices were in place at their school, and what their own idealistic ideas of trauma-informed schooling included. Additionally, I did some informal one-on-one interviews, which helped to inform and guide my work. Together, this was enough to capture valuable information to include in this book.

Some of the names throughout the book have been changed for privacy and confidentiality reasons. However, all stories or responses are authentic. These stories are meant to encourage you on your own personal journey. Each chapter ends with a short list of actionable items and helpful hints that I encourage you to try out. Some of them focus on self-care, while others are for the classroom, but all of them are meant to get your mind considering the whole body and mind approach to trauma-informed teaching and self-care. By providing case studies and practical ideas on how to improve pedagogy, and strategies for self-care, my hope is that this book will equip teachers with the information and skills they need to truly be effective for all of their students.

Below, I offer a brief overview of some respondents of the survey. You will also find a sampling of survey answers in the Appendix. I also highly recommend that you take about fifteen minutes to respond to the survey questions yourself, to get a baseline level for your own knowledge on these topics. Before you begin, know that there are no right or wrong answers. We are all here learning and wanting to do the best we can.

For example, Yoni, a young male of Indian descent attending an expensive private Franciscan Order college, is adamant in his idea and vision for trauma-informed schools. He believes that trauma-informed schools are schools that are committed to ensuring the success of all students in the classroom. He believes in providing equitable, differentiated means of approaching students regarding both content and well-being. Reading his responses made me want to jump out of my chair. He gave me hope, and lots of it. He's the change that will help our students thrive.

Jean, a high school principal, teaches in an urban district in Massachusetts. She describes the city where the school is situated as having the highest needs. Jean states that being a trauma-informed school means that all members of the team understand that the children bring with them the "unsettledness" that exists within their lives. Some stem from extreme crisis situations, while others may be more "quiet" and less notable. "Regardless of the level," she wrote, "these experiences unsettle the minds and the spirits of our children, which often causes them to not be prepared to focus on academic content, engage in social interactions in a positive way (with peers or with staff members), or to feel comfortable within themselves."

Carol, a veteran high school teacher of thirty-six years, insists that her idea of a trauma-informed school is one in which "the school considers what students and staff might be facing in their own lives. One in which all parties involved recognize the challenges and respond to the impact of traumatic stress." She continued by suggesting that "it is also a place where all students feel safe, welcomed, and supported." The response made so much sense considering that school should be one of the safest places for children. I've seen kids begin to "act up" before the holidays simply because they don't want to be in their traumatized homes or communities.

Anthony is white and grew up in a military family in Nebraska. He shared that, as a child, he moved often because of his parents' work, changing schools regularly and not having enough time to form relationships with other kids. In elementary school, Anthony was labeled a special education student. He doesn't think he was. He felt that he was targeted by teachers because he was taller than kids his age, had unruly red hair, and had an inquisitive mind. When he became a teacher, he thought of all the experiences that he had moving from one school to another, of his own students who had to move every time their parents moved, of the students in his classrooms who are refugees, and he vowed never to be like the teachers he had. Teaching for almost thirty years, Anthony enjoys his work in a school where the majority of kids receive free or reduced lunch. He describes trauma-informed schools as ones where kids are comfortable, and where he does not need to be controlling to be in control. They are places of positivity where he can engage their curiosity and imagination in a positive way.

The results of the survey, I must confess, did not come as a shock to me. There were no eureka moments. Instead, I discovered that most of the beautiful, creative, inspiring individuals surveyed reaffirmed my own experience: teachers desire to do the best for their students. However, they aren't necessarily equipped to deal with the myriad of issues that their children experience and often lack adequate skills and knowledge to compassionately care for and educate traumatized children.

For instance, Keturah, a high school special education teacher who grew up on the West Coast but now has a job in an urban high school, wasn't sure about her idea of a trauma-informed school. I loved this teacher's honesty, but her response made me question how she—and so many other teachers—were responding to the needs of traumatized kids in their respective classes. This book will undoubtedly provide some answers and support for Keturah.

In fact, as I paged through the responses, my heart became more and more conflicted. I worried about the children sitting before their teachers. I worried about my well-intentioned friends, some of whom did not demonstrate an understanding of the day-to-day grind of children living in high-density, high-poverty areas. It solidified my conviction that creating schools with thriving students isn't something we can do alone.

It's neither an understatement nor hyperbole when I say that the vast majority of individuals involved in educating our children require ongoing training and support in implementing culturally, ethnically, and linguistically trauma-informed inclusive curricula. In every conversation I've had on this topic, either in writing this book or in casual conversations, educators tell me that they need more authentic professional development training and guidance. They want to deliver trauma-informed instruction that incorporates Social-Emotional Learning along with state standard academic requirements. They also want to focus on their own health and well-being. With the ongoing mental health crisis among school-age children, the utter lack of adequate knowledge around issues of trauma and trauma response is unacceptable. Truly, there is no single person, or even institution, to blame for this situation, nor is seeking to blame a helpful course. If we instead focus on creating an awareness of this issue and implementing strategies to combat it, we can all rise together. And it begins with getting the teaching workforce properly trained.

The starting point must be determining where the staff baseline is. What do they know about adverse childhood experiences? What are their attitudes toward people of other races, ethnicities, socio-economic backgrounds, genders, and sexual orientations? What are their thoughts on out-of-school suspensions, Critical Race Theory, banning books, or even delivering instruction in a trauma-informed way? Trauma-informed schools acknowledge the racism, bigotry, classism, and ignorance that are inherent in so many education systems. Determining the knowledge of each staff member (as well as staff doing their own personal assessment) will identify areas of training and support that are needed. This also sets the precedent that everyone in a school community can commit or recommit to creating an environment where everyone thrives.

A hugely important piece of realigning schools to be trauma-informed is incorporating anti-racist curriculum school-wide, which includes high-quality professional development and human resource training. The anti-racist, anti-classist content must expose all staff to different perspectives, histories, and experiences, promoting empathy, understanding, and inclusivity. Opportunities must be presented to historically marginalized teachers to present at professional development trainings as these opportunities will be beneficial to entire school communities, including the presenters.

My Hope for You, Dear Reader

At my core, I am a teacher. I've done a ton of other important work in my life: I was a housekeeper, scrubbing floors and cleaning toilets on my hands and knees, and I did the three-to-eleven shift toiling at Hasbro Toy Factory making Busy Bee toys. I even worked picking up rocks! I was fourteen years old, with nothing to do one summer, when two of my friends told me about this job offer. It was to prepare a wealthy farmer's plantation for planting. I was paid pennies to spend all day in the hot, tropical sun picking up rocks and moving them from one part of the plantation to another. I've also knocked on doors in the Mount Hope section of Providence as an outreach worker. It was there in Mount Hope that I got a perfect glimpse of what poverty and trauma look like in the United States. It was that work and my relationships with marginalized community members that also influenced my desire to become a lawmaker.

Now you know that I'm a tough cookie with many experiences, but teaching is where so much of my joy lies, and it's where so much of my fight for justice originates. I get asked every day, "How do you do it?" First and foremost, let me categorically say that I'm not alone. God, the Almighty, helps and strengthens me for this fight. I'm also able to keep going because of the children. Their smiles and their joy, but also the pain in their souls that often make it hard for them to smile. I do it for them. I do it so that my grandsons and children in your respective classes can have a better experience in school than I did. I do it for all the little boys, girls, and non-binary children whom I will never know but whose teachers will benefit from this book. If through my work and the words in this book I can help even one teacher, one parent, one caregiver, or one child realize their own dream, then all the efforts poured into writing it will have been worth it.

I love my students and I want them to succeed. I want to pour into them what teachers poured into me. I was lucky to have teachers who were more than just educators. They were caretakers. Caretakers of a dream that one day a skinny little Black girl born and raised in poverty could one day become a teacher, an author, and a State Representative, wielding the power to influence and pass laws that would benefit all children, including non-binary, poor white children, children in foster care, and those who are often overlooked.

Teachers, the students in your classroom are not broken. However, they carry with them the trauma and toxic stress that represent failed government policies and systems that couldn't care less about their humanity. Systems that would rather build costly new prisons as opposed to new schools with the resources necessary to uplift our student populations. I have spent decades calling out broken government systems that have "othered" children and families living in poverty. I know that kids are hurting academically, socially, and mentally. It's the reason this book goes well beyond the traditional approach to teaching and learning, suggesting a pathway where emotional intelligence and academic intelligence flourish side by side. I'm tired of seeing so many of our brightest fail because of education systems that have failed them. This book is a call to action in creating transformative schools.

When I was young and still living in Jamaica, some folks looked at me and decided that I would amount to nothing. But I always had other ideas for my life. I had dreams of finishing high school, going off to college, and making my parents proud. I was willing to fight for my own survival and make something beautiful of my life. It didn't come easy. It had many twists and turns, personal setbacks, heartbreaks in between, but I made it! Today, I'm a full-fledged, purpose-driven Black woman who has risen from the ashes of shame, trauma, violence, and poverty. These days, I look in the eyes of my students and I see a field of dreams and untapped potential. I see hope. I see them defying the odds, just like me. I see them graduating high school and lifting themselves and their families out of cycles of generational poverty and trauma.

Deep within my students' eyes, I see the same hope, grit, and tenacity that I had. I see the zest for living and willingness to thrive amid all the drama and trauma in their lives. I'm reaching within the depths of my soul to help these children. I know you will too. I'm both a teacher and a learner. I teach the Common Core State Standards, but I also teach the lessons that life has taught me. I'm teaching my students how to overcome the odds and how to use the barriers in their lives as stepping stones to unleashing their fullest and brightest potential.

The job of teaching, especially in a core urban city, has been far from easy, but I will continue with every breath I take to teach, inform, inspire, and shape the world I want to see. This is backbreaking, and it tears at my heartstrings every day. Nonetheless, I'm committed to the pursuit of education equity. I'm driven to share my story, my resilience, my path to healing and thriving. I will continue to kindle the fires of hope and resilience, the fires of determination and ambition that lie deep in the souls of my students.

It's my sincerest hope that the anecdotes, illuminating case studies, and my personal story presented in this book will serve as a catalyst for personal and systemic transformation. Change is not always easy, but I'm hopeful that this heart work ignites a powerful, meaningful change and paves the way for school districts to be more supportive and caring for all children who enter their schools.

I also hope that my openness about my own story creates not just an acknowledgment of privilege for some teachers, but a greater understanding of working with children whose experiences may be analogous to their own. I share my lived experiences because I want you to know that the children who are in your classroom and who experience gun violence, systemic racism, and poverty can thrive with the right people and the right level of support. I want your interactions and your pedagogy to help students who experience trauma or post-traumatic stress disorders to be able to move from victims to survivors. They too can move to post-traumatic healing and growth. This book is a testament to my tenacious authorship in writing my own story, a script that continues with every heartbeat that resonates within me.

What will your story be?

PART ONE

UNDERSTANDING STRESS AND TRAUMA

CHAPTER 1

RECOGNIZING STRESS AND TRAUMA

I MET SIMONE when she was in my ninth-grade class. She had no formal education prior to coming to my school. She was a refugee from Afghanistan and had bounced around to several other countries and refugee centers before landing in Rhode Island. Despite the scars that were inflicted on her from years of mental, emotional, and physical trauma from going from one camp to another, from one country to another, she endured and learned to speak five languages. Kudos to her!

Simone was a beautiful girl, and while sometimes she was friendly and open, at other times she was withdrawn and barely spoke to anyone. It was clear to me that she had been through a lot, and she was having trouble adjusting to her new school environment. I made every effort to connect with her and to let her know how smart and special she was.

When Simone became overwhelmed or dysregulated, I immediately told my co-teacher that I'd take her for a walk. One day, through her sobs, she told me that she had been cutting herself and that it felt like the only thing that made the pain she was feeling go away. She also said that she tried drinking bleach to kill herself.

After listening to her carefully and asking a few questions, I gently hugged and comforted her. I then took her to the school's social worker and the school nurse, making sure she felt safe and comfortable with them before leaving her there. Once back in the classroom, I also made a written referral to get her a higher level of support every day at school. Listening to Simone's story was painful for me. My heart ached, but I was glad that we'd developed enough of a relationship that she trusted me with her hurt. I also knew that, given the right level of support, she could thrive.

Yes, Simone had experienced traumatic events in her life. She had seen war and was uprooted from her home, her culture, and everything she knew about her world. She was living in a cycle of stress and trauma, and when triggered, she would have outbursts in class, including uncontrollable crying. In another school and in another classroom that didn't have a teacher who understood and was willing to use trauma-informed approaches, this might have been seen as disruptive behavior and she could have been labeled a problem child. Instead, with daily follow-up and mental health services as well as home visits, Simone was able to get the support she needed and began to feel better. Her grades improved and she began to make friends. Through perseverance and a loving school community that responded to her needs expeditiously, she was able to graduate.

When someone is drowning, you don't try to teach them how to swim. You save them first, and once they've recovered, *then* you teach them how to swim. What I mean by this is that while we generally like to think of school as a place where children go solely to be educated, there is no compartmentalization for kids. They bring their whole selves everywhere they go, and while that may include their goofy personalities and inquisitive minds, it may also include the bad moments and difficult situations they've endured.

In instances such as these, teachers have a duty to refer the child to the Multi-Tiered System of Supports (MTSS) in your school, or, in the cases when this does not exist, most definitely to the social work team.

This chapter explores stress, trauma, and adverse childhood experiences, which are the context for what's going on in the mind and bodies of kids who may be "acting out," exhibiting attention-seeking behaviors, or failing classes. A note to educators—not all kids experiencing trauma will act out, display attention-seeking behaviors, or fail their classes. Quiet kids also struggle. These children may disconnect, withdraw, or dissociate from classroom activities. Teachers must not disregard these kids as such actions may be calls for help. Knowing your students and building relationships with them is a sure way to not only find out what they are struggling with but also to offer compassionate and personalized support.

The Three Kinds of Stress

The ubiquity of the phrase "I'm so stressed out" underscores the pervasive nature of stress in our lives. Indeed, stress knows no boundaries; it's an inherent part of the human experience. Stress in the classroom is not limited to students, either; and to understand our students' stress, we must reflect on our own. For me, balancing the responsibilities of being a mom, a wife, a teacher, and a justice seeker is quite stressful. Some of the stress comes from the day-to-day grind, while some comes from the sheer emotional toll from helping my own family and my students with the multitude of problems they have while often triggering my own "relationship" with trauma. This is not an experience I hold alone.

Meet Lorna, a lifelong social worker and friend whose dedication and compassion are qualities that inspire admiration and respect from those who know her. Lorna's passion, commitment, and centeredness make her a person you'd want in your corner during challenging times. She's always ready to employ her knowledge for the greater good. Yet even Lorna isn't immune to stress. Overwhelmed by a caseload of children in need and buried beneath an avalanche of paperwork, she often remains quiet.

One day, sitting with a cup of coffee amidst a mountain of paperwork, her eyes spoke a mixture of longing and concern. "Marcia, can we talk?" she inquired, lifting her gaze from her paperwork just long enough to ask the question. "Yes, of course," came my instantaneous reply. Instead of speaking, Lorna burst out crying.

"I can't do this anymore. I am overwhelmed. I am stressed out," she sobbed, her tears flowing freely. "I can't keep up anymore. The stress, the weight—it's too much." In that moment, Lorna, an adult, articulated her experience and acknowledged her emotions plainly. Due to her openness, we were able to talk out her very real concerns and find a way for her to move forward. But for many of the children we teach, such self-awareness may be elusive.

The National Institute of Mental Health defines *stress* as a physical and emotional reaction that people experience as they encounter challenges in life. When you're under stress, the part of the brain known as the amygdala reacts by releasing hormones that produce the fight-or-flight response. One's heart rate, breathing rate, and blood pressure go up, muscles tense, and sweating occurs. But believe it or not, all stress isn't destructive. Occasional stress is a coping mechanism, and our body's physiological response helps us regulate that feeling. However, long-term stress (also called chronic stress) may contribute to or worsen a wide range of health problems, including digestive disorders, headaches, sleep disorders, and other symptoms that necessitate attention. Unchecked stress may worsen asthma and chronic pain, and long-term stress has been linked to depression, anxiety, feelings of hopelessness, lack of sense of belonging, and other mental illnesses among both children and adults. Lorna was experiencing the physical pain of chronic stress and was ready to call it quits. This physical reaction is similarly felt in our students.

Stress is inevitable; it's part and parcel of life's tapestry. Life happens, and it isn't always going to be easy. However, there's a tipping point where stress begins to adversely affect the body and mind. This is the kind of stress that we must monitor in ourselves as well as in students. Within this context, let's delve into the three primary stress categories—positive, tolerable, and toxic.

Positive Stress

I see my little grandson, Elias, outside riding his scooter. He's as happy as a lark, riding along without a care in the world. Suddenly, he falls to the ground and scrapes his knees. Tears cascade down his beautiful brown cheeks. Rushing to his side, I offer a familiar voice and a gentle touch, "I'm so sorry, sweetie, let Gramma kiss your boo-boo."

Elias, hearing my calm and familiar voice, gets up but is still crying his eyes out. I remain calm, pick him up, kiss his knees, console him, and tell him that he's going to be alright. Like clockwork, the tears dry up, he jumps back on his little scooter, and off he goes down Waite Street, a smile lighting up his face.

Experiences that may be painful but are usually short-lived are considered positive stress. They are building blocks that occur as part of normal childhood development. In the example of Elias falling off his scooter, to him it seemed like the sky was falling when he bruised his knees. His heart rate became elevated and his body signaled the issue through pain. Crying was his way of letting me know that he needed me to respond to his physical needs. Of course, he wasn't badly hurt; he didn't even need a band-aid. What he needed was my comfort and attention. Once he received some kind words, a kiss on his boo-boo, and a hug, he calmed down, the stress response abated, and he was able to get back to the important stuff—riding his scooter!

For children, experiencing this kind of temporary and often transient stress is positive because it teaches valuable lessons. These experiences foster resilience, fortifying children to confront future challenges with renewed strength. Elias realized that although he fell and bruised his knee, it wasn't the end of the world. A minor fall won't linger in his mind and cause him to be afraid of riding. Plus, he knows that the adults around him are there to support him and lift him up if he ever falls. These kinds of stressors offer a chance for children to find inner strength and build their own reserves of determination, slowly learning that they can overcome challenges on their own. With love, care, and attention, all children can gain confidence in their own capabilities to overcome stressful times.

Tolerable Stress

Tolerable stress comes about when individuals encounter more severe or longer-lasting difficulties. This might be the loss of a loved one or a more severe injury such as a broken arm. These kinds of stress can cause physiological and mental harm, but they are often unavoidable. Providing love, care, and attention during difficult times will not stop children from experiencing these kinds of stress, but it will provide a buffer for them as they negotiate life's challenges. By helping children understand the situation and providing care, educators and caregivers can assist children to recover from traumatic events as well as help them develop resiliency.

Sometimes I look back on my own life and wonder, "How the heck did I make it?" The answer is resiliency. I was able to overcome much adversity in my young life because of the support from my parents, my church family, and my teachers.

Due to traumatic life experiences, many of the children we're teaching are psychologically, physiologically, mentally, and emotionally hurt or harmed. I often watch my students cope with adversity while attempting to power through the daily routines of school. Oftentimes, I'm in sheer awe, wondering how they carry on so well. Other times my heart simply breaks because they seem to be falling apart. I just don't know how these children get up and go, go, go. But, then again, I understand, I get it, I look in the mirror—they have their own personal dreams to fulfill.

As educators, we can't always intervene to get rid of situations causing students' stress. But we must try; we can help them to develop resiliency by teaching them how to identify and cope with stressful situations and feelings such as sadness, embarrassment, loneliness, anger, and anxiety. Lurline and I attended teachers' college in Jamaica, sharing a room in the small Franciscan women's college. Lurline now teaches in Brunswick, GA. Like me, she has over thirty years in education. In our phone interview, she tells me that she's never seen so many kids experiencing so many emotions, including suicidal ideation, as she sees today.

One way that she helps her students cope is by having them talk through what they are feeling. If there's conflict between students that's causing them stress, she meets with each student alone and gets their respective version of what happened. After listening to their grouses, she meets with all the parties together for mediation. In her meetings, she gives each child the norms of the meeting, including standards of behavior, followed by a review. First, students name the feelings that they are experiencing: "I feel hurt when you talk to me disrespectfully" or "I feel annoyed when I'm not taken seriously." Because saying things like "You did this" can feel confrontational, she models and encourages her students to use "I" messages, which frame the speaker's experience without invalidating how the listener might feel. She also uses role play to help children cope with stressful situations. For some students who become dysregulated, it's not always easy for them to see their classmate's perspective, but Lurline continues her efforts. According to her, eight out of ten times, she finds that these strategies work to help kids deescalate hurt feelings and emotions.

Tolerable stress is only tolerable if it's identified and regulated. That's why it's so important to be continuously watching kids for changes in their moods or behavior. This was made clear to me when one of my duties at a high school where I taught was as a morning greeter. It was one of my favorite responsibilities, and all it involved was standing at the school entrance and greeting kids as they headed to breakfast. For some, this would be the first meal they'd had since leaving school the day before. I will discuss childhood hunger and my fight to end it later.

I worked hard to get to know and greet kids by their names. This was intentional. I wanted each child to know that they were seen and valued. The responses on their faces when I said their names helped me to further understand the power that each of our names hold. If I didn't pronounce students' names correctly, I would ask them to forgive me and share my own story of how people would often pronounce my name as "Mar-sha" instead of "Mar-ci-ah." I would tell students that their name is their identity; it's where they come from, the food they eat, the songs they sing— their entire being. Knowing names and saying them correctly is an important part of relationship building.

I love laughing and dancing in the mornings at our school's entrance. Of course, I'm not naïve enough to think that just dancing in the entrance and turning up the speaker that one of the assistant principals, Ms. Walker, gave me is going to let all the stresses in our lives magically disappear. However, I firmly believe that children who are going through hardships, pain, and trauma deserve a reason to laugh, smile, and experience some level of joy. Seeing this modeled for them gives them permission to replicate it, and possibly to try to feel that way too. So, I was hellbent on making sure that the children I saw each morning had at least one thing to smile about. By dancing and laughing, I know I could set a welcoming tone for their entire day.

I had an opportunity in the summer of 2023 to share my joy of dancing with kids again. This time with elementary school kids at a summer program. Each morning, I began my day in the school's cafeteria. I noticed some behaviors that were not conducive to a healthy school environment. Kids were getting on each other's nerves, hitting each other, and engaging in minor squabbles. The behaviors were nothing excessive, but I felt that it created an atmosphere of conflict instead of collaboration. On cue, I began to dance. Soon the kids started dancing with me, some of the teachers joined in, and before long, our program was filled with joy and smiles all day. I can't say if it took away all the trauma from our lives, but it was clear that it brought joy and minimized the conflicts I'd previously observed.

You don't have to know exactly what children are going through to be a buffer for the stress they are encountering. Simply getting to know them, asking questions about their lives, and giving them the chance to engage in joy through dance or other activities can help kids weather the various storms.

I've seen that thirty minutes at the entrance of the cafeteria transform kids who were coming into school dysregulated. It's the little things that matter—a pat on the shoulder, a smile, a recognition that you're not just a student but a human being that's worthy of love, affection, and care. It's during those thirty minutes of dancing, talking, and taking selfies that I would learn what was going on in their young lives. In those moments, I would get to teach how I cope with tragedies, such as being gentle with myself.

I often say, to students and adults alike, "Be kind to yourself, speak nicely to yourself."

Just being there to chat every morning also encouraged kids to learn the skill of asking for help in a way that validates their strength. I tell them that some of the strongest people I know are those who ask for help. Another way to go about this is making sure kids see me asking for help from my co-teacher or other teachers. It could be trying to figure out a math problem or simply helping with the smartboard. I allow myself to become vulnerable so kids can see that it is okay to ask for and receive help. Life happens, we're going to get hurt, lose loved ones or our prized pet—and kids hurt too. It's important to remember that children are not exempt from their life experiences; they too face hurt and loss. Teaching our students healthy coping skills is paramount to them thriving.

It's easy when children are acting out or exhibiting attention-seeking behaviors to see them as broken or having some kind of deficit. The truth of the matter is that the children sitting in your classroom are like babies. Babies typically cry when they need a diaper change or when they are hungry. When a caregiver picks the baby up and attends to the immediate physiological need, the child becomes less fussy or may even fall asleep. Responding to babies' stress responses with soothing words and caring actions creates a solid and lasting foundation of trust. As the child grows, that trust follows them, but if it's broken by neglectful caretakers, it can develop into toxic stress.

Toxic Stress

Toxic stress comes about from constant or ongoing issues that activate the body's stress response systems. Usually, the response system remains activated until reprieve is initiated, but children living with toxic stress are in a constant state of fight-or-flight. In this frame of mind, and body, children often feel unsafe and don't have the bandwidth to think about classes or schoolwork. They are just trying to survive.

Children experiencing toxic stress may come from crisis-filled homes where they deal with a myriad of situations: an abusive or neglectful parent or guardian, coping with feuding parents going through divorce, or having loved ones who are incarcerated or murdered. This kind of stress is toxic because it's traumatic, ongoing without any relief, and beyond their level of comprehension. Children experiencing toxic stress don't need schools that feel unsafe or chaotic, or where teachers are often dysregulated and without adequate coping skills. They need schools that are trauma-informed, with caring adults who they can count on to begin breaking the bonds of toxic stress.

Miguel was only thirteen but he'd been through so much. He lived with his mom, who could barely keep the roof over their heads, and was hungry most of the time. Miguel met his father only once on a visit to Puerto Rico. A couple years after that visit, he learned from his mother that his dad had been shot and killed. The thought of his dad's murder haunted him. These unresolved memories catapulted him to seek refuge in attention-seeking and disruptive behaviors. One day, I watched Miguel sit in the back of class and kick the chair in front of him. Ron, the boy in front of him, looked around but did not respond. He was quietly doing his classwork and pretending to be unperturbed. Miguel upped the ante by pulling Ron's ponytail. Ron changed his seat, trying desperately to avoid confrontation.

I walked over to Miguel and said, "Miguel, please be gentle." He looked me up and down as if I were speaking another language other than English. With permission, I sat beside him, resting the palm of one hand gently on one of his shoulders. He didn't want to do his work, but as I sat by him, he began rocking back and forth in his seat. In this class, I was a co-teacher, so I could focus on this child while my co-teacher kept the rest of the class on track. Before long he was fast asleep. His behavior signaled to me that he was not only tired but also looking for some attention, and he'd take whatever kind came. By simply sitting with him, I made it clear that he had my attention, and he could finally relax.

Later that evening, I called Miguel's mom to let her know what had happened. She quickly responded, "I've had it with him. He's been getting into trouble since preschool, so I'm ready to send him back to Puerto Rico." My heart ached for this mom who was obviously at her wits end with Miguel. I connected her with a local parents' support group as well as referred him to our social work department for additional support and intervention.

When Miguel came in the next morning, I made an effort to meet him and had a quick check-in as I greeted kids coming into the cafeteria. I thanked him for coming to school and told him that I knew that he had missed some of the work from the previous day. "Don't worry about it, Miguel, I have everything you need, and I've reserved a spot for us to go through it today after school."

He smiled but said he wouldn't be able to stay since his mom expected him at home right after school. But he said he'd let her know my intent to help him, and maybe he could stay the next day. Like clockwork, he showed up the following day to get the work done. He also apologized to me for his behavior in class and said he would apologize to Ron as well. I asked him why he had been kicking Ron's chair. His response was revealing; he said the teacher had been going too fast and he didn't understand what she was doing. That frustrated him. We brainstormed some ideas and strategies that he could employ if he was getting agitated, upset, overwhelmed, or needed help in the future. Discreetly, he just needed to write me a note if he needed help and didn't want other students to hear.

Toxic stress lives in the body, but it also has to come out. Kids experiencing this kind of stress often fidget, are unable to concentrate, become disruptive, shift quickly into anger, or exhibit attention-seeking behaviors. In short, their executive functioning is compromised. *Executive Functioning* is a broad term that describes mental skills like paying attention, being able to sit still, organizing, planning, starting a task, being focused, self-monitoring, empathy, and being able to fully regulate emotions. When executive functioning is compromised, children may experience feelings of sadness or an inability to make healthy and thoughtful choices. Some kids may even resort to drugs, alcohol, or promiscuous behaviors as a means of overcompensating to help relieve toxic stress. In Miguel's case, he was desperate for attention but didn't know how to get the help he needed.

Instead of those unhealthy coping mechanisms, we can offer children healthy outlets and strategies for their feelings. I've seen after-school programs such as reading clubs, guitar lessons, chess clubs, open mic sessions, gardening, and sewing lessons help kids deal with their emotions in ways that uplift themselves and their school communities. As teachers, we may not be able to change children's circumstances at home, but we can let them know that school is a safe place where they can ask for help and they are seen and loved.

So Then, What is Trauma?

In 2019, after the full force of the pandemic had hit like a ton of bricks, I, along with the entire world of educators, was grappling with a new reality—teaching remotely. I could see my students were going through difficulties, including the deaths of family members and some periods of hunger and homelessness. Simultaneously, my mom was recovering from a massive stroke. The weight of these events bore heavily on me, exacerbated by the fact that I could only see Mom through the window of her home and my students through the screen of my computer. We'd all started feeling the effects of trauma.

According to the Substance Abuse and Mental Health Services Administration (SAMHSA), trauma "results from an event, series of events, or set of circumstances that is experienced by an individual as physically or emotionally harmful or threatening and that has lasting adverse effects on the individual's ability to fully function physically, socially, emotionally, and spiritually." This is different from stress in that trauma dramatically changes those who experience it. SAMHSA lists some types of traumas as:

- Neglect

- Psychological, physical, or sexual abuse

- Natural disasters, terrorism, community, and school violence

- Witnessing or experiencing domestic violence

- Commercial sexual exploitation

- Serious accidents, life-threatening illness, or sudden and violent loss of a loved one

- Refugee and war experiences

- Military family-related stressors, such as parental deployment, loss, or injury

Additionally, the National Network for Youth makes a point that trauma can come about from either real or perceived danger that's witnessed or directly experienced.

Trauma doesn't discriminate. In one nationally representative sample of young people ages 12–17, SAMHSA indicated that 8 percent reported a lifetime prevalence of sexual assault, 17 percent reported physical assault, and 39 percent reported witnessing violence. These numbers painfully translate into stories of children who are unprotected and exploited. Left unresolved, these types of traumas will snowball into lifelong adverse impacts such as drug use, mental and physical health issues, and homelessness.

There's no debate: trauma adversely affects the brain. The prefrontal cortex is where rational thinking occurs, and it regulates emotions such as fear responses from the amygdala. The amygdala focuses merely on survival, and the more hyperactive the amygdala is, the less the prefrontal cortex can rationalize whatever stimulus it encounters. The hippocampus is the part of our brain that's responsible for learning and memory. It helps us to differentiate between the past and the present, and with exposure to trauma, this part of the brain shrinks, thus compromising the brain's architecture. This restructuring is linked to signs of post-traumatic stress disorder (PTSD) because when stress stimuli are present, the hippocampus "remembers" past trauma and signals the same levels of reaction as those experienced during those past traumatic events. Expecting kids who experience trauma to react the same and follow the same rules as kids who haven't experienced trauma is like carrying water in a woven basket. It's not going to happen, because their brains have developed structures to over-react and under-control their processing of the world around them. So, there has to be a change in educators' mindsets and teaching strategies to account for these differences.

While stress isn't always harmful, trauma is. Trauma affects every system in the body, particularly the nervous system. Responses can be emotional (such as avoidance, denial, anxiety, lacking optimism, or depression) or physical (such as shock, self-harm, nightmares, trouble falling asleep, or illness). While it's normal to respond to trauma in a variety of ways, people can have difficulties moving past trauma responses and get stuck in a loop where they are experiencing and re-experiencing the same traumatic feelings. This then makes new learning very difficult. In the book *Helping Traumatized Children Learn*, the authors explain that "trauma can disrupt the ability of children to learn and process verbal information and use language as a vehicle for communication." I see this every day in children who come to school wanting to learn yet are crippled by the weight of trauma. The effects of trauma can also involve not feeling hungry, being unable to find or experience joy, extreme and sudden mood swings, disruptive behavior, and losing interest in school activities or relationships.

While everyone's response to trauma is different, the key indicator for children thriving amid trauma is having a caring school community where everyone—and I mean every single person in the building—feels safe, loved, appreciated, and valued.

Without proper mental and emotional care and therapy, trauma can be debilitating. Recurring trauma memories, ongoing stressors, family dysfunction, and all the awful things in between can interfere with a child's learning, behavior, and overall health and well-being. Left untreated, the effects of trauma can adversely impact young people's ability to be successful, plunging them into behaviors that can last a lifetime, like dropping out of school, alcohol and drug abuse or addiction, teen pregnancy, and self-harming behaviors. I've watched children over time who have been exposed to toxic stress spiral out of control into these behaviors. The worst part is that every time a child ends up going down these dark paths, their family, their community, and their entire world loses out on the positive and unique impact this child could have made.

Trauma in the Classroom

Going down memory lane, I recall being a housekeeper and dusting the same window-sills every day. "Cleo," I beckoned to the woman I worked for. "I just dusted this yesterday, so why is there so much dust again today?" She burst out laughing and, in her beautiful African American–Rhode Island accent, said, "Marcia, this is America. There will always be bills, dust, and stress." I kept on dusting.

For kids who get up every day and have to eat, live, and breathe adverse experiences, those experiences become a huge part of their lives. Without access to proper mental health intervention and compassionate care, all that toxic stress negatively impacts brain development and may lead to social, academic, and behavioral issues. I've seen children whose lives and homes are a constant source of stress and chaos. In places where there may be few or no rules and no order, it becomes extremely difficult for those children to adjust and conform to rigid classroom rules and norms. This isn't to suggest that they won't be able to adjust with time and patience, but it will take work. Children crave order and structure in their lives. I'll always remember Maylin, for example, who, when asked what she wanted most in her school, quickly responded, "Order."

To create order, a teacher must place student behavior into perspective. I often get asked by other educators, "How do you remain so calm when kids are acting so crazy or when kids are so disrespectful to you?" My answer doesn't always make sense, but the truth is that I don't take things personally. I don't think kids get up each morning and say to themselves, "I'm going to give Mrs. Ranglin-Vassell a hard time." It's not the kids—it's the trauma talking. If I can look at each situation through a trauma-informed lens, I know I will see a child who needs help and support, and I know attention-seeking behaviors are really calls for help.

Early intervention is also a key to helping children thrive. It's all our responsibility to intervene to help kids. They cannot do it alone and need a community of people who care, understand, and are willing to hold their hand as they negotiate complex trauma. Helping children develop stamina is possible by creating classrooms that uphold trauma-informed practices. Equipping school practitioners with the necessary tools needed to better assist students will ultimately help children cope as they enter adulthood and face more adversity.

Even in a safe environment, trauma will make itself known and may require more intervention than one teacher might provide. For example, take Travis, who'd been in and out of foster care all his young life. The only time he had what was considered "stable housing" was when he was caught driving a car without a license and sent to the juvenile training school. When Travis came to my classroom, he hadn't been in an integrated classroom in years and just didn't know about school or classroom norms. When given challenging classwork, he would often offer only profanity-laced outbursts. When asked to stop, he would create an even bigger scene by tossing chairs and yelling.

Travis didn't understand the rules and structure of the classroom or what was expected of him. He also felt threatened by both the routine and rigor, and the only way he knew how to handle something threatening was to explode. His feelings of confusion, frustration, and perceived loss of power triggered his trauma and led to his angry outbursts. Travis' behavior escalated with every passing day. The limited hours that mental health personnel were on-site posed a significant challenge for our school, especially in dealing with cases as complex as Travis'. His struggles often lead to situations where he felt "out of control," which put a strain on the meager staff to provide safety for everyone in the building, including this dysregulated child. Recognizing the gravity of the situation, the hard decision was made to transfer Travis to another school that offered more supportive services. I couldn't help but feel a sense of failure and disappointment. I felt that our school had let this child down. I had let this child down. But this situation highlights an important truth: one teacher alone cannot change the trajectory of a severely traumatized child. It takes a whole school community, a village pulling together, to meet that child's needs, and, sometimes, the ability to recognize when a child needs more than one community can give. Honestly, it's unfair to place myself or any other teacher in this precarious predicament of grappling with shoestring resources whilst a mental health crisis explodes within a child or soars nationally.

While any traumatic event that happens to a child may end, the experience lives on in their body and soul. Left unattended, it can haunt that child like a demon and constantly create havoc in their lives. I hear teachers complaining and labeling kids in a negative way all the time: "That kid is so bad," or "You have the bad group."

Let me state this unequivocally: there are no bad children.

However, there are children who may exhibit bad behaviors due to toxic stress and trauma. There may be kids displaying attention-seeking behaviors. There may be kids who have not been taught how to problem-solve or control trauma impulses through breathing or other mindfulness activities. There may even be kids who simply didn't receive the social training that they should have gotten during the formative years of their lives. Instead of casting blame and further humiliating or traumatizing kids, teachers can help kids negotiate the complexity of what's expected in the classroom by explicitly teaching, posting expected behaviors in classrooms, sticking to routines, having morning meetings, and modeling desired behaviors.

Here's another example: Jordan was a teen in one of my classes who desperately wanted to do well but had an issue with organization. Every day, he would rummage through his backpack, trying to locate his work. He became fixated, taking out one sheet of paper at a time, looking it over to make sure it was the correct one. Jordan would lose valuable class time just rummaging through his book bag for that one handout lost among all the other things in his bag. This would lead Jordan to become overwhelmed to the point of shutting down, leaving the class, or getting sent to the principal for lashing out. It didn't take me long to realize he had struggles with executive functioning.

Jordan didn't have an easy life. He'd been abandoned by his father and bounced around from one foster home to another, never in one place long enough to put down roots. He'd been in many schools, all with their own rules and expectations. One thing he always had was his backpack, and he kept everything in it, including food and extra clothes. I think it helped him feel safe, but it wasn't very organized or conducive to keeping worksheets.

During our advisory period together, we would sit and not only go over the classwork that he needed to finish but also how to organize using color-coded pocket folders. This kept him from becoming overwhelmed when he couldn't find a particular assignment. The intervention to support Jordan was pretty simple but helped his trauma response. This invariably helped him to remain in class and become more productive.

As you can see from the scenario presented, there appeared to be multiple issues impacting the learning of this child. Because trauma is a real and pervasive issue among youth of all ages and zip codes, there has to be a structural shift from a punitive model of fear and punishment to one of healing, love, and compassion. Classrooms should be safe spaces where kids can explore new ideas, make mistakes, learn from them, and thrive. Classrooms should support all children where they are at, instead of harshly disciplining the ones who are struggling or acting out.

Unless safety is an issue, my goal is always to keep children in the classroom. Sending disruptive children away to be disciplined doesn't teach them what's appropriate classroom behavior—they can't replicate what isn't modeled for them. Instead, I ask myself, "How can I redirect their attention and energy?"

Inadvertent Diagnosis for Special Education Services

Each child's response to trauma, toxic stress, and adversity will be different. I've seen a wide range of responses: fear of trusting people (even those individuals with the best intentions), loss of hope that anything good will happen to them, loss of faith in themselves, shame, guilt, withdrawing or distancing, sadness, anger—you name it, I've seen it. (I've also experienced some myself.)

What I've also seen is what I believe to be the inadvertent misdiagnosis of many children in special education. Many of these diagnoses are placed on children because of behaviors or responses that are triggered by trauma.

In my years of experience in education, I've seen where kids are labeled "Emotionally Disturbed" or "Learning Disabled" when all they needed was additional social-emotional support. This isn't to assert or even imply that most children receiving special education services are inappropriately placed. Instead, it aims to highlight the pervasive bias not only in testing procedures but also in the targeting of minority and poor children in the foster care system and in schools for special education services. My thoughts here are not intended to "throw shade" on the amazing work of psychologists or other members of your district evaluation teams; however, the issue calls for a closer examination and for urgent rectification. I think there needs to be a forensic look and deep dive into some of the culturally biased tools that are used to evaluate children from diverse backgrounds who enter into school systems that are unprepared for the complex trauma some of these children harbor in their bodies.

The impact of child poverty, the pandemic, the housing crisis, as well as the mental health crisis nationally have only exacerbated the problem of referring kids to special education classes. In some case, all some kids need is love, support, and comprehensive wraparound services to include family support. Increasing special education numbers might seem a good way to provide more services, but it inadvertently creates bigger caseloads for teachers and an overload in a system that already lacks human resources to adeptly manage the influx of new and possibly miscategorized students. An overburdened system also takes away valuable time and resources from kids who would benefit the most from these specialized services.

Yvonne is a parent who once told me the story of her son, who was deemed special ed and given prescription medication to calm him down. She knew that he acted out simply because he wasn't challenged in his public school. She refused to give him the medicine and worked with him outside of school. With the help of caring teachers who saw how smart he was, he was able to finish high school, go on to college, and is now a successful engineer. Though perhaps his story is the exception rather than the rule, it does show that each child must be looked at individually and cannot be diagnosed just based on their outward behavior alone.

Another pervasive issue in special education is racial profiling. Unfortunately, in the case of Black and brown children, special education misdiagnoses stem from a racially biased system that continues to traumatize them throughout their schooling. A Harvard Graduate School of Education article I read during my research postulated that "students of color are disproportionately sent to special education to their detriment, isolated in classrooms with teachers who have less expertise in important subject-matter material like math, English, and science." My years of experience in education certainly made me aware of this too, since I myself have been relegated to the basement to teach my special education students a subject I had not been trained in. I firmly believe that in order for us as a society to break generational trauma, there has to be a shift in the manner in which children of all races are evaluated, assessed, and placed. I also think it's important that we have highly qualified teachers in respective content areas teaching classes.

Part of this involves Diversity, Equity, Inclusion, and Belonging training (DEIB) for school psychologists, social workers, and other members of evaluation teams. While well-intentioned, some of these people may have no idea about the lived experiences of children of color and the structural challenges they face. I don't for one moment underestimate the fact that there are children of color who need medicines, therapy, counseling, and other mental health services. However, we cannot and should not stigmatize children based on race, ethnic background, or socio-economic status.

Helpful Hints from Teachers

- *Utilize the power of reflection.* Go back through your day either by thinking about it, talking it through with someone, or writing about it and examining what happened. What went well? What went wrong? What can you change for tomorrow?

- *Fall in love with yourself every single day.* In order to better serve your students, you must call upon the best of yourself and let that shine through.

- *Withhold judgment.* You never know how high a mountain kids are climbing.

- *Use the bathroom before the bell rings!* Even the smallest disruption, like calling administration to cover your class, can trigger a traumatized child.

- *Get to know your trauma team.* Every school should have a counselor, social worker, or substance abuse counselor. If they don't, advocate to have them on board.

CHAPTER 2

ADVERSE CHILDHOOD EXPERIENCES

I GREW UP IN A community overrun by poverty and gun violence. I was witness to more traumatic experiences than most reading these pages have seen or heard about. I saw dead bodies lying on the ground during my formative years. These were the bodies of people who were mercilessly shot and killed. They belonged to family and friends, people who I laughed with, played with, and ate dinner with. I watched my own family's two-room board house viciously vandalized by people I grew up with. I experienced hunger as a child. I endured sexual assault as a high school girl.

I wish I didn't have to think about those experiences that have invariably shaped the person I am today, but I don't have that luxury. They have become part of my permanent memory, my brain's architecture. So why am I sharing some of these stories publicly for the first time? I'm sharing these now because the people who harmed those I loved, who perpetrated violence against me and my family, and who sexually assaulted me no longer have power over me. I refuse to be a victim. I'm a survivor. I've been through a lot, but I've survived. I'm healing. I'm thriving.

My sharing is twofold. One, I want school teachers and staff to know that children in your classroom might have suffered the same or similar fate. I'm sharing this to let others know that they can rise above the ashes of violence and sexual assault trauma to continue with their lives. As proof, my presence here is not mere coincidence. I could easily have been a somber statistic, another Black woman falling victim and dying due to a system that's rigged against her, leaving behind a trail of trauma for my children, grandchildren, and those who love me. However, through writing, I have come to realize that hidden in all the traumatic things that have happened in my life, ultimately, I've found clarity, meaning, and purpose. I've found and will forever be enveloped by joyful resilience. The shame that I've carried for decades no longer has power over me. I've reclaimed my agency and my power. Most importantly, I've rediscovered myself, but complete healing is an ongoing process that will take time.

In many Black and African American cultures, including my own, there's a negative stigma around accessing mental health services and care. Taboo around this issue, as well as mistrust of medical systems, complicates Black and African American people seeking care. This fear of betrayal is real and rooted in centuries of systemic betrayal by those who have tricked us into believing they would be our "saviors." One need only go back to the Tuskegee Syphilis study or the atrocities that poisoned families in Flint, Michigan, to gain a better understanding of the mistrust of systems by Black Americans and people of African descent. This history in itself is traumatic; however, we must explore therapy and healing that acknowledges our fear and mistrust, and one that can help assuage the fear and trepidation.

I mention this in part because being able to help children living with trauma also means that you'll have to deal with your own trauma. Personally, I struggle with the issue of trust, and it has nothing to do with me liking or not liking a person. I like people—in fact, I love people! I think this fear could stem from betrayal; I haven't been able to figure that out quite as yet, though I'm working on it. My fear includes not being able to fully attach to people outside of my family, and attach to things, including prized possessions. If I have something that someone else says they like, I will immediately offer it to them without a thought. I believe that it's because I grew up poor, so I hardly had anything that was my own, let alone things that were new or pretty. They were always hand-me-downs that I would probably be expected to eventually give to someone else, so I never attached myself to things. These are some of the vestiges of trauma that I will forever be working through, including the effects on my mental health.

In the last year, I have endured the deaths of three women in my life: my beautiful mom, my aunt, and my sister. These losses have been difficult, and I'm still in grief. It took the pandemic and the loss of my cherished mom on her birthday before I picked up the phone and reached out for mental health services. Before that, I remember seeing a mental health counselor maybe twenty-five years earlier. Things have been difficult, I must confess, but my power comes in part from deciding that my experiences could be a guiding light for me and those around me. My own struggles hold the keys to connecting with students whose lives mirror my own. I navigate the often-grueling path of reliving some of my own traumatic memories in an effort to hone in on the healing elements of my journey and forge a pathway to new and transformational learning. In this way, the things that make me feel alone, tired, sad, or vulnerable become my strength.

It hasn't been lost on me that I went through life not having a name for some of the horrible things that seemed so normal in my life. But now I know they are called *adverse* childhood experiences (ACEs). According to the Centers for Disease Control and

Prevention, ACEs are any potentially traumatic events that occur in childhood (0 to 17 years). ACEs include but are not limited to experiencing or witnessing violence in the home or community, abuse (physical and emotional), divorced parents or loved ones, neglect, bullying, having a family member attempt or die by suicide, poverty, hunger, systemic racism, and homelessness.

While not all of the traumatic occurrences that happened to me were in my formative years, cumulatively they have influenced the person I am today. In fact, for young children, these experiences can have devastating impacts on life's trajectory if left unresolved. In her article "Childhood Adversity: Buffering Stress & Building Resilience" for the American Academy of Pediatrics, Nerissa Bauer writes:

> *Our body has systems to protect us so that when faced with a scary situation, we are ready to run and hide. This "fight or flight" response can be triggered whenever a child is scared of any number of things such as dogs, the dark, or spiders. This same system can also be turned on when a child experiences any adverse experience. However, ACEs are likely to last longer than a single moment, which causes children's stress systems to be turned on for a long time. When this happens, the stress becomes "toxic" to their overall health.*

As discussed in Chapter 1, the physical body and the brain are changed by traumatic events, but when trauma is experienced daily, as in the case of ACEs, those changes can dramatically impact a person's well-being. Educators, administrators, paraprofessionals, custodians, cafeteria staff, bus drivers, and everyone on the team must pay keen attention to the students in our care and offer help and support to them as well as their families.

Let's examine a few ACEs—childhood hunger, school shootings, systemic poverty, and COVID-19. These issues, some of which are historically pervasive and some of which are now front and center of our lives, are impacting school children at epidemic proportions. In addition, smartphones and social media usage, while not exactly an ACE, are issues that constantly come up at school. By understanding what adverse childhood experiences are, school personnel can maneuver the complex issues children face, learn how to respond to them, and practice self-care simultaneously. Because every child is unique and every issue is different, addressing them requires skilled, compassionate, trauma-informed awareness, interventions, and care. It's my hope that every school has a student support center that works with the entire school community and is willing to share resources to connect kids to in-school or direct community resources.

Systemic Poverty and School Attendance

One may ask, "What does systemic poverty have to do with school attendance?" Turns out, everything. In an article "Why is School Attendance Important? The Effects of Chronic Absenteeism" published by the School of Education at American University (2021), American University utilized US Department of Education data to support the argument that school attendance is a powerful predictor of student outcomes and, according to the department, "irregular attendance can be the best predictor of whether students will drop out of school before graduation than test scores."

I teach kids who have been absent from school for upwards of 40 of 180 days. Providence Schools reported this data in a recent board meeting, and Steph Machado, in an online *Boston Globe* article titled "Half of Providence Students were chronically absent during 2022-2023 School Year," noted:

50 percent of students were in school 90 percent of the time in the 2022–2023 school year. That means 50 percent missed at least 10 percent of the year, meeting the criteria for chronic absenteeism. Put another way: more than 10,000 students each missed 18 days or more during the most recent school year.

Of course, these numbers are atrocious. We need our students in class every day, ready to learn. So why are these students absent? Many believe it's because of a lack of motivation on the part of the student, but upon closer look, one can see that systemic poverty is a driver of attendance issues.

Let's peel away the layers from the onion. Even if a student's family doesn't fall below federal poverty lines, kids are absent from school for a myriad of reasons and we should never assume a student just isn't motivated to attend. For students living in poverty, it may be that their economic circumstances force them into chronic absenteeism. For example, most students in my school district receive free or reduced meals, which means that most students' family income falls below federal poverty levels. Such designation refers not only to the likelihood that students will be hungry but also as an indicator of adverse childhood experiences. At the high school level, ACEs may take the form of added familial pressures. It's no secret that many students living in the urban core work out of necessity. They must help their families pay rent and keep groceries in the cupboards. Students are also skipping school and staying home to take care of younger siblings if their parents are absent due to illness or work responsibilities. The American University report not only corroborates my claims of why students are skipping school but also provides some additional information: "Compared to peers who graduate, students who fail to complete their high school education are more likely to live in poverty, suffer

poor health, and become involved in the criminal justice system."
It doesn't have to be this way and can be prevented by robust and
equitable government intervention.

Poverty also ties into the issue of transportation. Many parents don't have cars or are already working when students need to
get to school. When we speak of absenteeism, we must not forget
children living in rural areas who are poor and who don't have
access to reliable or accessible public transportation. Others in
urban communities may not qualify for free transportation due to
mileage restrictions.

Chronic homelessness is also pervasive in populations with
a lower socio-economic status, so some enrolled students leave
school in the evenings without the faintest idea of where they will
lay their heads at night. In this country, where the 1 percent stash
exorbitant wealth they will never be able to spend in offshore accounts, kids in urban, suburban, and rural communities go to bed
without food in their bellies and with no place to call home. When
students are homeless, they are also less likely to attend school,
and when they are in school, they have a hard time focusing on
learning due to their heightened levels of traumatic stress.

To illustrate the impact of ACEs related to poverty, I want to
share why I keep Simba's list for groceries on my end table. Simba,
a brilliant eleventh-grade student, didn't want much; he scribbled
his list on lined paper and passed it to me: French fries, Hamburger
Helper, chips, Cap'n Crunch, meatballs, mash potatoes, grapes, mac
and cheese, apple juice, bread, peanut butter, string pasta, baked
beans, apple sauce, and tacos. He'd confided to me that he, his
mom, and his little sister had been using the food pantry at their
local church, but the church was seeing an increase in the number
of people utilizing the pantry, so they had to limit the number of
days per week that a family could go for emergency food. Tearfully,
he told me that his grades were also falling because he stayed up all

night worrying that the landlord would put the lock on their doors; hence, when he came to school, he fell asleep. Other times he would be absent from school. It wasn't that his mom, a single parent, didn't try—in fact, she worked two jobs—yet with the rising cost of rent, she was sinking deeper and deeper into poverty. On another occasion, after Simba had built more trust with me, he confided to me that he and his mom were struggling really badly, and they were also facing eviction as their rent had more than doubled. Every night before I say my prayers and retire to bed, I take up Simba's list to remind me why I fight to end childhood hunger and poverty.

The harsh reality is, for children across this country and around the world, there's no escape from painfully traumatic economic circumstances. It's a daily reality, especially when you are living with systemic poverty. Despite being aware of the adverse childhood experiences associated with poverty, school systems everywhere are devoid of robust and adequate social and mental health services to address the critical and complex needs of a student population of a lower socio-economic status. To me, this is a particular failure of the government to respond to children in crisis. How sad that Rhode Island is not the only state struggling to meet the demands of the mental health crisis that accompanies poverty. We know a solid education is the first rung on the ladder toward a better life, so how can we get these students to show up to school every day and keep showing up ready to learn? It begins with understanding what they are experiencing and knowing how to recognize signs of trauma. Most importantly, educators need to have tools and strategies ready to respond.

Childhood Hunger

One morning when I was co-teaching in Mrs. Stuart's tenth-grade statistics class, I noticed Kelvin with his head on the desk. This was out of character for him. He loved math and was usually jostling with his classmate Samantha to raise his hand and answer questions. On this day, he was withdrawn and wasn't engaged at all with the problem set that the rest of the class was working on in small groups. I knew something was wrong. Sometimes children who experience trauma can be withdrawn, but this wasn't usually the case with Kelvin.

Without disrupting the ecology of the room, I walked over to check in on him. "Hey Kelvin, how are you?" I asked. "I see you're putting your head down. Are you not feeling well?"

After a long pause, he looked up with an air of both disgust and embarrassment and muttered, "I'm hungry, Miss."

At that moment, I couldn't help but think of all the times when I went to school hungry as a child. Of course, Kelvin couldn't concentrate; he was hungry, and he couldn't have cared less about learning math that morning. The truth of the matter is that food is a basic human right, and no one, especially children, should ever go without food. Not allowing myself to dwell on the past or revisit the trauma that I'd experienced, I told him to wait. Hurriedly, I went to the cafeteria to get some breakfast for him. He sat silently eating his muffin and banana and drinking the small carton of milk with cereal. Before long, he was like a withering plant that had just gotten a dose of water. He was ready to work. What I did was nothing spectacular or magical, it was simply recognizing that the student needed food to concentrate and getting him what he needed.

Many children experience what is called "food insecurity," though I just call it hunger brought on by failed government policies that keep children in deep poverty. I don't feel the need to sanitize my words when it comes to injustice or inequalities simply to make others feel comfortable. When I get an unexpected, unsolicited text from a student saying he or she needs food, or hear about a mother who's been evicted and is now held up in a hotel without food, I do not see this as food insecurity; I see this as children and families being traumatized by the circumstances that they are trapped in. I see this as our collective shame.

According to a *Time* magazine report, the number of children living in poverty in the United States more than doubled in 2022. Children not having food in their bellies makes it extremely difficult for them to focus or concentrate on what's being taught. It can also lead to a student exhibiting disruptive behaviors or even academic failures, which could further the cycles of generational poverty.

In Kelvin's case, his inattentiveness could have been construed as a lack of respect, leading to disciplinary actions—effectively punishing a child simply for being hungry. Instead, making sure Kelvin had food in his stomach so he could get back to his education was an easy resolution. I know how difficult it is for teachers to teach and pay attention to everything that goes on with every child in front of them. However, our vigilance could be the key to making sure children get the nutrients they need for growing minds and bodies.

As educators, taking the time to acknowledge that you see something wrong and letting kids know that you care is the first step. While providing one meal doesn't solve the systemic problem of childhood hunger, it helps students to feel seen and valued. It also builds that important relationship which opens the door the next time a student needs help. For further information, you may refer to my *Boston Globe* commentary found in the Appendix section of this book under the heading: "With So Many in RI Living in Poverty, School Meals Should Be a Priority."

School Shootings

My journal entry on March 14, 2018, reads: *"Overwhelming day today. Apprehensively, teachers and students huddled in different corners of the front of the school yard to honor the lives of the 17 students that lost their lives in Parkland."* At that time, and now, my mind wanders overseas to my neighborhood back home and to all the folks that I, too, have lost: both family and friends. It's hard for me not to think of them anytime I hear about another senseless gun death. My trauma recurs at times like these, and this will be a part of me for as long as I live. Just as I lost my innocence to the grief of gun violence in Jamaica, my students' innocence was taken by the totally preventable school shooting and mass murder of innocent children at Parkland. We will never forget.

Now, consider the Uvalde shooting, where twenty-one children and two teachers were killed by an evil twenty-one-year-old shooter. The surviving children and the mourning families need decades of prolonged and competent mental health services and therapy to help address their scars. With each new announcement of such mass shootings, I begin thinking of all the students that I lost to gun violence in Providence, too. Though these are not large-scale publicized tragedies, they are still extremely traumatic to the communities in which they happen. They traumatize me as a school teacher, and they definitely traumatize our students and all school staff, thereby qualifying as an ACEs factor. We will never forget.

We cannot and should not normalize school shootings. This type of violence is unacceptable and a symptom of a broken system. Children should be able to go to school without worrying about getting shot and killed. Educators and staff working in school buildings should also be able to have workplaces where they aren't sitting ducks waiting to be shot, maimed, or killed.

Gone are the days when the only thing we had to practice was fire drills. Even those were traumatizing. Now, we have active shooter drills. Are we in a war zone or what? Evidently, we are. Though it's important to be prepared, even practicing the drills can be traumatizing for children who've experienced ACEs, especially those who have been exposed to acts of violence involving guns. As part of planning for safety drills, school administrators should consider children for whom these events might be especially stressful and make sure teachers and counselors are ready to assist as needed. Mental health services for children and staff alike are necessary to lift the emotional burden of experiencing and reliving this kind of trauma.

Schools are sacred places, and this is why I spent much of my time as an elected official fighting to pass school-specific gun prevention laws. For example, I co-sponsored and successfully passed legislation, now Rhode Island law, to limit the number of people with firearms on school grounds. The Harold M. Metts School Safety Act of 2021 "prohibits the possession of firearms on school grounds except for peace officers, retired law enforcement officers, persons under contract to provide school security services, and unloaded firearms in locked containers or a locked rack on motor vehicles." The implication of this law is far-reaching and will most certainly protect children's mental health and well-being. I also think that it's vitally important that teachers and staff are knowledgeable of state laws so that they can at least have a sense of safety and security. Of course, even as we continue to do better, there needs to be a federal response to gun access. I'm not in any way trying to restrict the laws that are on the books, such as the Second Amendment law. I'm simply stating that we need to do a better job as a country to protect the mental, emotional, and physical health of our children and staff, as well as protecting lives.

The COVID-19 Pandemic

As in many places across the country and the world, the shutdown of schools happened really fast in Rhode Island. Without much notice, on March 18, 2020, then Governor Raimondo, now Secretary of

Commerce in the Biden Administration, announced that all Rhode Island schools would be utilizing a distance learning model for the foreseeable future. For my district, which already struggled with poverty and gun violence, the pandemic only added stress to a school community that had seen more than its fair share of trauma.

The impact of COVID is devastating, far-reaching, and ongoing, creating havoc in our children's lives. According to Children and Youth Cabinet, an organization serving Rhode Island's children, data gleaned in mid-2020 from nearly 3,000 students indicated that 78 percent of students had someone close to them who was very sick or injured, 86 percent experienced loss or separation, and 45 percent experienced a natural disaster. All of this, compounded with the added tension and frustration of distance learning, only helped to worsen the mental health of children. Therefore, the pandemic qualifies as an ACEs factor.

I, for one, hated the new educational format as it meant I was essentially disconnected from my students. Teaching over Zoom put a damper on my chances of effectively connecting one-on-one with students. It was also much harder to tell how kids were doing or what they needed help with through a screen. And, of course, for kids living in poverty, the impact was even greater. There were issues of internet access and connectivity equity; I would spend hours on Zoom waiting for students to show up. Often, my students couldn't join me because they had no internet access. It was and continues to be a struggle to ensure that every child has access to reliable internet regardless of their zip code. Distance learning also meant there were no more snow days. Personally, I think this is a bad decision, as kids and teachers would benefit from more mental health days, more time to play in the snow, and more time to de-stress.

Once we were back in school after two years of online classes, educators had another challenge on their hands—the re-socialization of students. While it was a blessing to have kids back in school, it came with significant challenges related to inadequate mental health support. The truth is that many kids have lost so much due to bouts of hunger, homelessness, and isolation. Many students had also abandoned the social skills needed to cope with the rigor of school in favor of pure survival. In other cases, kids struggled to find footing in schools that had become foreign to them.

I witnessed kids who didn't have to speak directly to an adult for two years struggle to have simple conversations that required eye contact or even a few minutes of dialogue. I saw kids not wanting to hold their heads up, not wanting to make eye contact with each other or with adults. The truth is that for two years, children were not required to have those social interactions, and when they did during the pandemic, they were in masks. Now they were forced to return to traditional socialization and didn't know how. It made them uncomfortable to be put in that space, and many disappeared into their phones just to feel safe behind a screen again. My heart cries every single day as I witness the struggles of students who grapple with finding appropriate ways to interact with teachers, school staff, and their peers.

A study by the Centers for Disease Control and Prevention (CDC) found that the percentage of children ages 5–11 seeking mental health care at emergency departments in 2020 increased by 24 percent from 2019. For children ages 12–17, mental health-related emergency room visits increased 31 percent. The really tragic part is that there aren't enough mental health professionals to assist children, especially in high-poverty schools. Rather than improving, the problems are only getting worse.

Stress and stress-related issues were also inflamed by children living in a constant state of uncertainty. Kids who shouldn't have had to even think about things like their parents losing their jobs or dying were confronted with those fears, and sadly it became a reality for many of them. A *Newsweek* article from February 2022 estimates that, at one point, over 200,000 US children had lost a parent or caregiver to the pandemic. I've seen the sad reality of children I know who have lost family, neighbors, and friends to the virus.

Consider Alty, a sixteen-year-old who attended a local high school and lived with both of his grandparents. Alty didn't know his parents but seemed content with his grandparents, who adored him. Prior to the pandemic, he was a happy camper: very social with friends and almost everyone at school. Alty was a straight-A student, and everyone who knew him, including his teachers, had high hopes for his future. Then, his grandmother died during the pandemic, and things started plummeting. Alty became withdrawn, didn't practice personal hygiene, and only communicated through his phone. He had put up a barrier and hardly talked to anyone, including me. His schoolwork slipped, and although his grandfather tried, Alty was totally disengaged from the rest of the world. A referral to the social worker's office didn't help. He'd become selectively mute. Alty was showing signs of depression, his self-confidence had waned, and now he spent most of the class period hiding under his hoodie. The school continued to support him through its social work department, and an outside referral was activated to support this young man. We have students like Alty in schools all across the US and globally. Placing more psychologists and mental health counselors in all of our schools is the only way to arrest this heartbreaking problem.

Phones and Social Media

With COVID-19 prompting extreme isolation and increased use of social media, kids' mental health has been compromised because students now do most of their connecting through screens. The US Surgeon General 2023 advisory supports this assertion when it states that "Social media among young people is nearly universal, with up to 95 percent of teenagers, and even 40 percent of children aged 8–12, on social media." The same advisory also warns that extensive use of social media platforms is harmful to preteens, teens, and young adults. Therefore, kids who are allowed too much screen time may be exposed to adverse childhood experiences (ACEs) via their phones.

The use of smartphones in the classroom is not just disruptive to a child's learning, it also changes the culture of the classroom. Personally, I find myself in a complex web of emotions when I contemplate the prospect of an outright ban on smartphones in schools. On one hand, I see the problems of teachers like myself wanting to teach without competing with the allure of smartphones and social media platforms. During my tenure in the legislature, I joined forces with other legislators advocating for banning smartphones in Rhode Island public schools. At the time, part of my thinking behind this ban was that online interactions can put children at risk for harm, including human trafficking. Interacting with social media can perpetuate body dissatisfaction, low self-esteem, and disordered eating behaviors, especially among teen girls. The unfortunate thing is that kids are spending way too many hours each day on social media. Prolonged exposure, I believe, can lead to symptoms of anxiety and depression.

But the stark reality of school shootings has given me a conflicted heart. The very real potential of kids needing a way to contact emergency services or family makes a phone ban feel wrong. In addition, for some kids from historically marginalized groups such as LGBTQ+ communities, kids and youth with disabilities, or kids who don't feel connected to school, smartphones may provide opportunities to connect with others to find like-minded support. It appears that we're all caught in the "web," and the fight to limit screen time to protect our students' mental health, gain their trust and respect, and provide high-quality instruction remains tied up in complications.

Mental Health as a Determinant of Student Outcomes

Navigating the stresses and traumas of life is challenging for grown-ups. So, it's a sobering thought to consider how we expect children to handle similar pressures without adequate care and support. The harsh reality is that students are ill-prepared to handle the stressors and hardships placed on them, especially in a "post-pandemic" world. Their developing minds and bodies aren't adequately equipped mentally, physically, or emotionally to handle it, especially when those minds and bodies encounter repeated ACEs.

Kerri was an only child. She had dark, piercing brown eyes that seemed distant and filled with pain. I wanted to take her home every time I saw her walking the corridors at school. She had lost many of her close friends to gun violence, and though her mom had done everything to support her, she was never the same after those losses. Kerri was a nervous wreck, her mental health had deteriorated, and it was now impacting her physical health. She was suffering from chronic migraine headaches that made it difficult for her to concentrate in class and engage in the rigor of classroom activities. The hallways, always quiet and calm while classes were going on, became Kerri's safe zone. It was in the hallways that she could try to escape from the physical and emotional pain she felt. But time spent in the hallway meant she wasn't receiving the education or instruction she needed to get ahead in life.

I made space to have a safe conversation with Kerri and learned that her father was arrested right in front of her. As her teacher, I was able to comfort her and provide space when she needed to rest in class. I was also able to refer her to both the psychologist and social worker, who "tag-teamed" in their support. But not all schools have enough mental health resources or personnel, which in itself is a tragedy.

In April 2022, the Rhode Island Chapter of the American Academy of Pediatrics, the Rhode Island Council of Child and Adolescent Psychiatry, Hasbro Children's Hospital, and Bradley Hospital declared a state of emergency regarding children's mental health. This came after the 2021 release of Rhode Island Kids Count Issue Bulletin data showing that one in five (19 percent) children ages 6–17 had a diagnosable mental health problem, and one in ten (10 percent) had significant functional impairment. Further, only about 22 percent of high school students reported receiving the help they needed when feeling anxious or depressed, which was down from 33 percent in 2019. These statistics signify the urgency of addressing mental health support and resources for children and adolescents.

Unfortunately, this coincided with state mandates that school leaders and school administrators prioritize standardized testing. This pressure to prove the worth of education inevitably meant placing children's mental health on the backseat. This was the wrong time since the harmful effects of trauma caused by ACEs have been exacerbated by new post-pandemic societal demands on children. The resulting mental health crisis has led to a rather heartbreaking increase in the number of kids taking their own lives. According to the National Institute of Health, "Most people who die by suicide have struggled with a mental health condition. Other risk factors include a family history of suicide, violence, or substance abuse. Teens also experience many stressful life events, which predispose them to dying by suicide. Some of these events include a breakup with a romantic partner, trouble at school, violence, or conflicts with friends." Being a teen is hard enough. Couple that with more adverse experiences, and children are struggling. These are only some of the unfortunate and devastating realities that teachers must contend with while dealing with their own trauma or mental health issues.

Over the years, I've gone to several funerals of children who have taken their own lives. I've consoled my own children who have lost their friends to suicide. I've had students who have expressed thoughts of suicide to cope with the trauma that they cannot escape. The real epidemic—a mental health epidemic—is growing every day. For Black youth, the suicide rate has increased over the last decade, becoming the "second leading cause of death in Black children aged 10–14," according to the National Institute of Mental Health (NIMH). The director of NIMH, Joshua Gordon, also stated that "Black people face increased rates of risk factors, including experiences of racism, higher rates of unemployment and financial and food insecurity, disparities in other aspects of health, and limited access to care, all of which result in an increased burden of mental illness in Black communities."

In addition, according to Rhode Island Kids Count, "socioeconomically marginalized children and adolescents—for instance, those growing up in poverty—are two to three times more likely to develop mental health conditions than peers with higher socioeconomic status." This means that systemic racism and systemic poverty—often issues that intersect—are causing children to develop mental health conditions that negatively affect their outcomes at school and can even cause their death.

While mental health crises in our schools rise, school-based mental health services are diminishing. With limited services, the bulk of the work supporting students both academically and emotionally now rests on teachers, many of whom are dealing with their own stress and trauma. It behooves us to equip school personnel with adequate resources and ongoing professional development training so they can recognize and expeditiously respond to children in crisis. Caught between a rock and a hard place begs the question: what are educators supposed to do with the crisis in mental health that has only festered and escalated?

These first two chapters have offered a basic foundation for understanding general stress, trauma, and adverse childhood experiences (ACEs). But there's more to the picture. Next, we'll address racial trauma and its connection to generational trauma, which are issues that have plagued Black, brown, Indigenous, and other people of color since America began.

Helpful Hints from Teachers

- *Love all children like they are your own.* This means loving them through their difficult behaviors and disruptions and really seeing who they are underneath.

- *Find time to connect with kids,* knowing that this may require a different technique for each of them.

- *In the classroom, having space where kids can engage in academic rigor as well as space where they can play games, draw, or rest is valuable.* The simple act of supplying fidgets that kids can quietly use at their desks will help kids self-regulate and feel supported.

- *Become a Mental Health First Aider,* for which a certification course is offered through the National Council for Behavioral Health. This valuable training equips educators with essential skills and knowledge to support kids dealing with thoughts of suicide or emotional dysregulation, as well as kids just needing help negotiating their feelings and emotions.

- *If you're a survivor, don't wait like I did.* Don't hide because of shame or worries of repercussions. I urge you to speak about it when you're ready, in a confidential setting and with folks you trust. Please seek the appropriate physical and mental health services to help guide you through the traumatic memories that you'll undoubtedly encounter.

CHAPTER 3

RACIAL AND GENERATIONAL TRAUMA

I'D JUST TURNED twenty-six when my teaching career began. What I'd hoped for since I was six years old was finally happening! I was a full-fledged teacher, bells, whistles, and all! My first job was working with special needs children at the School of Hope for the Mentally Handicapped. Soon after, my friend and college roommate, Jean, enticed me to come to the school where she'd already accepted a teaching job.

John Mills All Age School was nestled in a quiet corner diagonally across from a recording studio. It wasn't unusual for children to stand at the barbed fence and gaze at the popular artists, including The Honorable Robert "Bob" Nesta Marley, going in and out of the studio. The kids hoped to get a glimpse of the King of Reggae himself. The Reggae beat pulsated from every corner of the studio, and the kids giggled, moving to the music. I bet it offered a silent reprieve from the harsh reality of having to walk up and down Retirement Crescent and into the concrete jungles to get home.

It was at John Mills that I realized it didn't matter where

poor children live; their experiences are the same. Many of my students came to school hungry, and still others had to walk or run through dangerous areas, risking their lives from gunfire. But once they were at school, what mattered most was how they were nurtured. In those early years, I learned that children can and will learn, given the right pedagogy and caring adults to support them. When children are enveloped by love and warmth, their capacity to flourish is exponential.

After four years of teaching, I moved to Rhode Island, where I did odd jobs, from cleaning houses to working in a factory. Moving from Jamaica to Providence was such a culture shift and shock. Everything was different. Everything.

Fate shone on me, though, and after years of being denied the ability to teach, I secured a teaching job at the Bridge Alternative School, which was intentionally located in the Urban League, in part because of the wraparound services available to students and their families. This was the place where they sent all the "bad kids" for periods of up to forty-five days to continue their schooling. It was a one-room schoolhouse where high school kids ages 14–21 all learned together. In forty-five days, I was supposed to wave some kind of a magic wand and the kids would be "perfect." After their time at The Bridge, as it was affectionately called, the kids were expected to transition back to the regular setting. In some rare cases, administrators thought the kids were "so bad" that they were refused re-entry and would stay with me for the entire school year. Despite those outward assumptions, I knew the kids weren't bad, and I would often see myself in them and some of their struggles. Without a doubt, I knew they were worth so much more than they'd been told or made to believe.

Most of the students attending The Bridge were boys—poor, adjudicated Black boys. A smaller percentage were Hispanic, and yet a smaller number were Asian boys, sprinkled with a few girls.

All had been through the judicial system for one reason or another and attended the Center for Hispanic Policy and Advocacy, or the Urban League of Rhode Island alternative schools. Both agencies had been the centers of the Latine and African American communities, respectively, for decades. The organizations were trusted, so it was easy for families to send their children to them, knowing that they would be properly taken care of. In addition, the agencies provided wraparound services including GED acquisition, childcare, emergency food, and re-entry services for families getting out of prison. Unfortunately, both agencies folded due to a lack of leadership, leaving many children and families without a reliable safety net. Luckily for kids who run afoul of school rules of behavior, a similar school has been set up to support them.

While working at The Bridge, I bore witness to the poignant pain and loss my students endured. It was at The Bridge that I saw firsthand, up close and personal, what racial and generational trauma is. Kids were now sitting in front of me whose grandparents were incarcerated, whose parents were incarcerated, whose cousins and aunties and uncles were incarcerated. Other students were part of the newest generation of families living in extreme poverty. Now, these beautiful children had the weight of that history on their shoulders, and not a single one in their immediate family knew how to turn their generational curse into a generational blessing.

What I found both interesting and revealing was that issues from home weren't discussed in the classroom. I think that the children, despite all having experienced similar things, were taught to be silent and feel shame for the violence and struggle that their families went through. All that tension and stress just bubbled below the surface—until it erupted through fighting or other disruptions in class. Teaching at the Bridge School was not for the faint of heart. It required grit, compassion, and determination. Here I was teaching kids, many of whom had lost hope in a school system that had failed them, turned on them, and turned them out. The Bridge was, in many ways, their last hope of getting a high school diploma, dodging the Adult Correctional Institution, or even staying alive. It was, in fact, a bridge of hope. I took this hope with me when I left the Bridge School, which was closing, to teach in Providence Public Schools.

Every day, I get out of bed and feel both privilege and gratitude to teach in the city of Providence. Providence is the largest school system in all of Rhode Island, with, according to its website, a population of 19,403 children. It has a very rich and beautiful tapestry of students coming from all over the globe. The district serves approximately 69 percent of students who are Latine, 14 percent Black, 6.5 percent White, 4 percent Asian, 5.5 percent multi-racial, and 1 percent Native American. The school district reports that approximately 40 percent of students are multilingual learners, and 17 percent receive special education services. It's a district where nearly 55 percent of students come from homes where English is not the primary language spoken. Providence proudly boasts that students and families speak a combined fifty-five different languages and hail from ninety-one countries of origin.

The teaching staff, however, is not representative of the student population. I'm among the handful of Black teachers of the 2,000 teachers. I'm also one of only a handful of teachers who actually live in Providence. That, in itself, is a gift because I'm able to see my students and their families everywhere I turn: in church, at the park, or even smiling at me as they check out my groceries at the supermarket. This allows me time to see and speak to families without having to wait for a scheduled meeting or having to call on the phone. It also gives children an opportunity to have someone at school who lives next door to them and understands the struggles of what they are going through.

Every day, I showed up wanting to make a difference in the

lives of the kids sitting in front of me. In that one room at The Bridge, which served as a gym, cafeteria, and classroom all in one, I learned from personal experience that they were more than the trouble that had landed them at the school. But not everyone felt that they were more than the trouble they were getting into. I remember Sandra, a middle-aged white woman who traveled from Connecticut to teach in our community. She had a beautiful smile and a contagious laugh, but she couldn't see past her prejudice toward the kids. She didn't have any experiences that allowed her to relate to their struggles, and she didn't live in their community, so her assumptions fueled her bias.

One afternoon, as we got ready to plan out the next week's activities, Sandra blurted out, "I'm not sure why we are even going to meet, all these kids are going to end up in prison anyway." My jaw dropped. I couldn't believe what I'd just heard.

I was filled with anger and blurted out, "I don't want to talk to you anymore, and I certainly don't want to teach alongside you."

I stormed out of the room, called Harry Porter, director of the program, and told him in no uncertain terms that I didn't want to work with Sandra. That was the last time I saw her. I'll admit that wasn't the best way to handle the situation, and I now wish I could have sat down and had a conversation with her about her racialized biases.

The point of this story is that when we say that students are bad, not worth our time, or going to end up in prison, it's like we're putting them in that cell ourselves and throwing away the key. For Black and brown students, they are coming to us not just with book bags filled with books, but book bags filled with complex trauma. Their identities, forged from living in a racialized and racist society, cannot be separated from who they are as students. Their whole selves come to our classrooms, as well they should. As teachers, we must take that identity, that history, and that trauma into account when we teach. And most importantly, we cannot begin the conversation of trauma—especially when thinking about children—without having conversations about race and privilege. In this chapter, I will take a look at some specific intersections of race and the schooling system to make it clear how racism, racist policies, and racialized trauma disproportionately affect children of color and their chances for a better future.

A Racialized Society Means Racialized Trauma

Kimani is a young Black teacher living and working in one of the poorest communities in Massachusetts. He had a tough upbringing, experiencing trauma in his own life, but with the help of a mentor, he was able to get to a place in his own healing journey where he can now help children like him.

Kimani shared an experience with me I won't soon forget. He recounted working in a school district as a special education teacher. The school had a student population of over 80 percent children of color. He recalled his department having weekly meetings, and he was the only Black person, the only person of color, with five other white staff members. They would often infuse a bit of humor to lighten the meetings, or they would ask him questions about his experience as a person of color. Not a problem, he thought. He suspected that to remove the stress that often shrouded the meetings, every now and then they would candidly talk about the issues of race and their collective response to combating racism. One day, he recalled the meeting taking a sharp turn. A social worker, an older white woman whose job was to provide counseling care to students, blurted out, "There is no racism in America." The silence in the room was deafening.

Kimani couldn't help but interrupt the silence. "Yes, there is," Kimani responded, "and I'm witness to it every day." At that moment, he said he knew it wasn't the place to get into a back-and-forth with the counselor, so he didn't.

After school, he sent her an email saying that he wanted to talk to her more about the issue. Instead of talking to Kimani, the counselor doubled down, responding that her parents came to the United States from Ireland and were discriminated against based on that identity. Her reasoning was that her family was just as impoverished and discriminated against as the Black students' families. By doubling down, she refused to acknowledge systemic issues dating back to the time of enslavement of Kimani's ancestors—something that her family would never have had to deal with. She never took the time to listen to Kimani, to hear his story or perspective as someone whose experiences aligned with the children he taught.

There's no question in my mind that this teacher failed to recognize her own privilege, truly thinking that the struggles her family went through were the same as the struggles of the Black teacher's ancestors. How easy is it to pass judgment on an entire race? How easy is it to even acknowledge the history of others?

The old saying "You can't fix something unless you can name it" is true. Racism exists. We all have ingrained biases from living in this society. A sure way to unlearn those biases is to actively listen to the perspective of others. See issues from other people's perspectives and be willing to unlearn myths and stereotypes. This is hard and intentional work, but it's both possible and liberating. So, it's important for all of us to have uncomfortable yet loving conversations about race if anything is going to change for our students. A part of that change is acknowledging that racism in America contributes to trauma, suppressing students and damaging their chances of breaking cycles of poverty. Actively listening with an open mind, with empathy, and without interrupting the speaker is a good way to speak and learn about race as well as how to be anti-racist. As educators in schools where there's not enough representation of Black and brown teachers, I believe it's critically important that we acknowledge our own biases, continually seek out opportunities to learn about race and ethnicity, and confront the systemic issues that interfere with teaching and learning.

So, what is race? Race is, first and foremost, a social construct. It can be described as the physical traits shared by a group of people with common ancestry. Regardless of the circumstances (voluntarily or forcedly) that remove immigrants from a particular region, country, or continent to another place, it's impossible to separate an individual from their race. After being stolen from the coast of West Africa, my ancestors were deposited like cattle in a place called Xamyca (Jamaica) to work as slaves on the land. Of course, this was after Christopher Columbus massacred the Caribs, Arawaks, Tainos, and all Indigenous peoples living on the island. The truth is, I'm a Black woman, a Black teacher, a Black mother, a Black person living in America. Here I am at the end of that long, horrible journey through the Middle Passage where my enslaved ancestors were sold and traded. I still bear the scars of that horror and trauma. However, over time I've had to confront my own hurt, biases, and blind spots as I seek to advance equity for all, regardless of race.

I don't have the space to unpack the history behind slavery and racism in America; there are many good books that focus on this, including *Stamped from the Beginning* by Ibram X. Kendi and *Caste* by Isabel Wilkerson. The point I want to stress is that folks are dying because of their race. This is a fact. Black people—Black children—are dying just because of their skin color. Emmett Till, Trayvon Martin, Tamir Rice, Michael Brown, Sandra Bland, Breonna Taylor, Botham Jean, George Floyd, and so many more whose names we will never know but in whose memory we continue to fight.

All of the tragic murders that were committed in what has been categorized as a hate crime, from the parishioners at the historic Emanuel African Methodist Church in Charleston, North Carolina, to the ten Black people at Tops Supermarket in Buffalo, New York, all died because they were Black, plain and simple. I think of the children in Uvalde, Texas, mostly Latine, along with their two teachers, who were hunted and killed by a white supremacist. This isn't rocket science, and you don't need a PhD to see that the color of one's skin has far-reaching impacts on people and their ability to stay alive.

Consider the trauma, exhaustion, and constant fear that Black children feel. When Breonna Taylor was murdered in her home, a ninth-grade girl told me how scared she was, wondering if she too was going to be shot and killed. How was she supposed to focus on classwork when this kind of fear was consuming her? And what could I say to make her feel better? As a teacher of a predominantly low-income majority of children of color, I was scared not only for myself but also for the children and their families. No one should have to live like this.

America must come to terms with the trauma it has intentionally and forcibly inflicted on African Americans and people of African descent, including folks from the Caribbean. This trauma is particularly focused on those of a darker skin hue. To be Black and brown in America is often not being able to send your child to a high-performing school. To be Black and brown in America means being denied the basics, such as clean running water, or having to breathe toxic air due to environmental racism. To be Black and brown in America is to be profiled, hunted down, and shot to death while jogging in your neighborhood, shopping for groceries, or simply existing. It's not enough for white people to say that they are not responsible for the evils and the sins of their foreparents. It's not enough for white teachers to claim "wokeness" while enforcing the very system that has inflicted trauma on so many of their students. It's not enough for white social studies and history teachers to only teach Black history during February or gloss over the few pages that reveal Black enslavement while glorifying the parts of history that make their ancestors saviors. We must all do better.

The Generational Effects of Trauma

Something that goes hand in hand with racial trauma is generational trauma. The *Washington Post* reported that this kind of trauma "can stem from biology, learned behaviors and even the collective experiences of a group. Some research suggests that trauma can affect a person's DNA and potentially influence the health of future generations far removed from the traumatic event." Generational trauma can be caused by a single traumatic event or a combination of adverse childhood experiences, such as drug use and abuse, rape, incarceration, poverty, racism, or suicide.

These unresolved psychological wounds are passed down from one generation to another, perpetuating harm along the way and suppressing the potential of grandparents, parents, and children alike. Seeking out a certified mental health professional is crucial to breaking the cycle of generational trauma, thus paving the way to healing and growth among families, including children.

While generational trauma affects people of all races and ethnic backgrounds, its most profound impact is observed in families whose ancestors have experienced forced labor, abuse, neglect, torture, rape, oppression, starvation, enslavement, and other harmful atrocities. These experiences and many more disproportionately affect enslaved people and continue to affect their descendants. In addition to the trauma that's embedded in their DNA, Black folks from the diaspora who live in the United States still face significant social, economic, and educational barriers that have been passed down from generation to generation.

These barriers are evident in our public school system. For example, public school funding relies mainly on property taxes, which is why schools in poor neighborhoods receive less funding. This automatically creates an unequal system since property taxes in affluent and wealthy neighborhoods are significantly higher and populations are lower, meaning schools in those districts end up with more money per student. Consider also that in high-poverty areas, the concentration of children living in poverty, children receiving free or reduced lunches, multilingual learners, newcomers to the United States, and those receiving special education services are higher. Therefore, it would make perfect sense for these schools to need more funding to begin with, yet they often receive less.

Black and brown students are more likely to live in less affluent neighborhoods and attend schools with inadequate funding. Due to this systemic inequality, the vast majority of students of color are starting out lower on the academic ladder than their white peers, thus widening the education gap. Disparities in education funding also have far-reaching consequences on children's social, emotional, and academic outcomes. Relying on property taxes to fund schools is tenuous, furthers inequality, and widens the wealth gap. School systems must also do more for poor white children, and they must do more in the social and economic infrastructure of lower-income communities in order to build stability and resilience.

It's also important to note that some states, such as Rhode Island, don't legally consider education a right. Rather, it's a capitalist concern, and the focus on the financial elements of education reinforces affluent districts getting better quality supplies and enticing teachers away with the promise of better salaries and working conditions. As a public school teacher in Rhode Island—a state that once harbored the largest slave port in the western hemisphere and which, until recently, was officially named "State of Rhode Island and Providence Plantations"—I see the vestiges of slavery in our education system. The implications of this injustice mean that the wealthiest Rhode Islanders can send their children to private schools or highly funded public schools while the state's poorest children languish in lead- and mold-infested classrooms without adequate resources to catapult them from cycles of generational trauma and poverty to health and well-being.

The way the stress of this generational trauma influences kids can be difficult to parse, but here's an example: I was helping to teach a group of ninth graders when, all of a sudden, Kaitlyn began yelling and swearing. It wasn't at anyone in particular, but she wouldn't let up. Not wanting to disrupt the general education teacher who was in the midst of teaching or the other kids who were busy studying *Romeo and Juliet*, I walked over to Kaitlyn and tenderly asked her if it was okay for us to go for a five-minute walk so that she could regulate her emotions. She responded with an air of utter defiance, "I don't f*cking care! My mom dropped out of school, and my dad was kicked out of every f*cking school until he dropped out. I don't care. I'm going to drop out of school too, don't talk to me, f*cking get away from me."

She had become dysregulated and lashed out because she didn't know what else to do. In situations like this, educators must remain calm, use soft tones, and show profound empathy. I didn't want to escalate the situation anymore, and I didn't want to add to Kaitlyn's dysregulation or perhaps trauma memory. Because I didn't yell back or reprimand her, Kaitlyn was caught off guard. She realized I was unmoved by her profanity and agreed to go for a quick walk with me. As we walked around the perimeter of the school, she told me that she was upset with her parents; her dad was incarcerated, and her mom wasn't interested in her welfare.

She told me that, listening to the teacher talking about *Romeo and Juliet*, she kept thinking of her mom and dad and how they had brought her into a life of uncertainty. She was worried that her fate was going to be similar to that of her parents. I listened attentively and thanked her for trusting me to tell me how she was feeling and what was bothering her. I reassured her that I, along with several people in the building, would help her to change the trajectory of her life and that she had my full support.

Although she may not have named it as such, part of what Kaitlyn was struggling with was the weight of generational trauma. She articulated this through her worries that she felt she was in the same trap as her parents and would end up having the same issues they had. The situation felt unfair and overwhelmed her to the point that she couldn't focus on what was going on in class. Taking the student for a quick walk to help her regulate her emotions may be all that can be done when students are in crisis. In Kaitlyn's case, it worked.

Later that day, I met with the school mental health counselor and described what I heard and my response. Although Kaitlyn's behavior would generally warrant disciplinary action, I chose not to write her up or refer her to administration for further action. I didn't think that going down the punitive route was the solution. I chose the better option, which was to seek care and support for her. We worked on a plan to get Kaitlyn time to talk through her concerns. By the next day, Kaitlyn was back to her usual friendly self and participating in class. To further support the student routine, check-ins were added to her "care plan."

Kaitlyn's story is also a great example of how ACEs connect with generational trauma. In a 1998 study of more than 17,000 patients, mostly white and middle class, the study funded by the CDC and conducted by Dr. Robert Anda, an epidemiologist at the CDC, and Dr. Vince Felitti at Kaiser Permanente, explored the connection between ACEs and trauma by tracking the effects of childhood trauma on health throughout one's lifespan. One of the significant findings was that ACEs were a contributing factor to past, current, and future health behaviors, social problems, and even death. "Ongoing research in neuroscience and epigenetics made it clear that ACEs have a neurological impact, often across generations. This impact ripples through individuals' health outcomes throughout their lifespan, serving as a fundamental contributor to numerous adult physical and mental health challenges." The clarity of this evidence demands a resolute societal commitment to dismantling generational inequities among marginalized populations as well as communities impacted by other social and economic ills. At the very least, every child should be able to grow up in a world where they can flourish and reach their highest potential and abilities, regardless of race, gender, ethnic background, or zip code.

As more individuals in the profession enroll and take an increasing number of classes on trauma-informed practices, there's a question of whether they're effectively translating this knowledge into classroom realities. Despite the growing availability of professional development classes and courses around understanding ACEs and trauma-informed practices, more actionable growth is still required at every level of the school system. This isn't a judgment on educators who are all making every effort to be more thoughtful and compassionate in our interactions, but it's a call to action for school district leaders and, quite frankly, for all of us to acknowledge the reality that complex trauma holds immense weight, and scientific evidence backs this claim. Fusing what is learned into practice becomes even more important with the rise in the mental health crisis.

The Mental Health Stigma as a Result of Generational Trauma

Everyone has periods of stress in their lives—it's inevitable. No one is immune to stress; however, Black families have dealt with the burden and stress of systemic racism, exploitation, and bias for centuries. Child Trends captures it perfectly: "Virtually every facet of the lives of Black people in the United States—both adults and children—is shaped by race. America's racist laws and policies have long impacted Black Americans, regardless of their socioeconomic status or social standing." Accessing care for many of us in the Black community isn't easy as it involves negotiating many systemic and structural barriers.

The stigma associated with accessing mental care, especially among people identifying as Black or African American, has made it increasingly difficult for us to seek out and receive treatment. Specifically, there's a stigma in our community that suggests reaching out and seeking care might mean that one is weak or even a little "crazy." Sadly, this stigma has been passed down from one generation to the next.

When I lost my mom in the height of the pandemic, I was struggling emotionally. My mental health was in a shambles. I was teaching and taking care of kids who were struggling, yet I was failing to access mental health services. I just didn't want to go. I refused to interact with a system that, deep down, I knew had betrayed people who looked like me. Thankfully, there's an erosion of this stigma, especially as prominent Black Americans are publicly speaking out and sharing their own struggles with mental health. These high-profile celebrities include former First Lady Michelle Obama, who's helping to destigmatize mental health struggles. I'm grateful for this, but there's still work to do.

It's not a coincidence that people identifying as Black Americans are less open to accessing mental health services. There are structural barriers, such as lack of insurance. But even if you have insurance, you may only be able to access providers who do not have the lived experience of racism or the training to work with people seeking racial healing. While I firmly believe that all mental health workers can provide skilled, caring, and competent care, representation matters. Being seen by someone who understands your particular struggle matters. The same is true in our schools. School districts must do a much better job to recruit, train, and retain mental health workers who not only have lived experiences but also share the culture, values, and expectations of the children that they care for.

From a young age, Black children learn to mistrust authority because they contend with elevated levels of scrutiny, discrimination, and over-policing, as well as disproportionate rates of out-of-school suspensions. The American Psychological Association (APA) stated that "for Black students, unfairly harsh discipline can lead to lower grades." These distressing factors not only elevate their stress and trauma but also systematically deny them equitable access to opportunities to be socially and academically competitive with their more affluent peers. This makes it all the more difficult for Black students to cope with mental health challenges and the stigma associated with it.

The APA underscored the alarming disparities inherent in disciplinary procedures. In a 2021 study, a comprehensive analysis was conducted on a dataset spanning three years of school records. The dataset gleaned information from disciplinary records and grade point averages for a total of 2,381 sixth-, eighth-, and tenth-grade students. The students were drawn from twelve schools in an urban mid-Atlantic school district in the United States. Of the students, 818 were Black and 1,563 were white. In addition to the statistical analysis, the researchers also surveyed the students each year about their perceptions of their school's climate, such as whether they felt they belonged at the school or whether they felt that school rules were consistent and clear.

Notably, the findings unveiled a striking disparity across the span of three years: 26 percent of Black students received at least one suspension for a minor infraction compared with just 2 percent for white students. Minor infractions included things such as dress code violations, inappropriate language, or using a cell phone in class. Furthermore, the research indicated a notable link between the imposition of suspensions and academic performance. Not surprisingly, as noted above, Black students who were subjected to suspension had lower grades.

It doesn't take much to see the connection here. Black students receive more punitive attention than their white peers and it negatively affects their grades, which negatively affects their futures. My frustration often reaches fever pitch when people, especially those that hold the reins of power, refuse to connect the dots and continue to harm Black, Latine, and other students of color by unfair exclusionary and punitive practices that are rooted in systemic racism. There's not a shadow of a doubt: structural poverty and systemic racism coupled with acts of violence that children experience stymies their overall growth.

One of the first bills I introduced when I served in the Rhode Island General Assembly was to reduce the number of out-of-school suspensions. Keeping kids out of school because of minor infractions deprives them of both the skills and knowledge they gain in the classroom. In addition, it further disenfranchises them from an education and sets them up to fail and enter the school-to-prison pipeline. As educators, our responsibility is to respond with love, care, and understanding to ensure that all students feel seen, supported, and valued.

I look at the faces of the children sitting in front of me and see myself staring right back, their eyes filled with hope and resilience. They are rambunctious and beautiful. Their smiles permeate the classroom, and for a moment, they can see beyond their generational trauma to a future where they are thriving. This is what we should all be working toward.

Poverty Is a Policy Decision

Poverty and trauma are interconnected. In Jamaica, it wasn't about race. Instead, it was more about class. It was so ingrained in the culture that there was no need to talk about it: you were either rich or dirt poor. There was nothing in between. Your class and trajectory in life were determined at birth. Unless your parents were wealthy enough to send you to private schools like Hillel Academy or Priory, or you were lucky enough to pass one of those hard-hitting exams set in London, your only choice was to be stuck in an under-resourced, low-performing school.

Honestly, when you're poor, not many people give you the time of day. I hated being poor. I loved my parents but hated the fact that they were poor. So much of the trauma that I experienced—and still experience—comes from my economic circumstances. I won't soon forget how embarrassed I was growing up, wearing hand-me-downs and walking to school without shoes. I'd hide from Mom when she came to parent-teacher meetings because I didn't want to associate myself with her. Of course, it didn't matter to me that my parents worked extremely hard to put food on our table and clothes on my back while denying themselves necessities. I appreciate their sacrifices now; it's because of their strength that I'm able to rip up my predetermined narrative and write my own story. It's what I've tried to do with my own children, and it's the lesson I give to my students every day. You can write your own story of triumph.

Every aspect of a child's development and well-being is tied to their family's station in life—physical, mental, social, emotional, and economic, and there are children in your classroom right now who come from generations of poverty. This is why I'm so resolute in trying to help kids escape poverty and to set them on the path to success. I'm not the only one doing this. So many educators are simultaneously doing the same, but we need more to. This is a call to action for educators to see the inherent value in every child and work intentionally and with compassion to help that young person thrive.

The reality is that poverty, like race, is a social construct. It's based on bad policy decisions made by people in power who, for the most part, don't care about those living on the margins of society. I'm still not sure why, in the richest country on the face of the Earth, families are surviving on shoestring budgets, working forty to eighty hours per week, some having two or three jobs, and still living in poverty. Reader, this isn't quantum physics. When there's robust investment in the infrastructure of schools, as well as bold investments in small and micro-businesses, families are able to help not only themselves but also their children. Government can and should commit to doing these things to help break cycles of poverty.

I met Alana in 2014, my first year as a special educator. I knew that she and her sister were being raised by their mom, a single mother who worked odd jobs to make ends meet. Alana was a smart girl, but she was always in the assistant principal's office for some reason or another. One day, she was having a really bad day at school and was becoming more and more dysregulated. Like many times before, and many other upset students before, I decided to take Alana for a walk to calm her down. As we walked up and down the stairs, she leaned over and whispered, "Miss, my sister and I are homeless. We're sleeping on the floor in my other sister's house. We are poor, Miss." My heart sank listening to her. I saw myself reflected in Alana's eyes. My parents had nine children, and we had a single full-size bed. As we got older, we would go over to my grandmother's house to sleep, sometimes on her floor. I suddenly understood why Alana had been acting out.

Children come to school to learn. They should never have to worry about where they will lay their heads once the last bell rings. The sad reality is that the odds are stacked up against children in classrooms all over this country and worldwide living in poverty. Unfortunately, I've heard well-intentioned teachers blame their students or call them unintelligent for being unable to read or do math. I've heard well-intentioned teachers call children names or reprimand them for disruptive behaviors. I've seen students get suspended and sent home when they are simply crying out for help. How often do we ask ourselves: could this be linked to childhood poverty?

We cannot lose sight of the fact that childhood poverty often stems from public policies established and perpetuated well before the start of this country. Proof of this lies in who is more likely to be poor. According to the Children's Defense Fund, "systemic racism and institutional barriers mean that children of color have been particularly vulnerable to child poverty. Black and Hispanic children experience some of the highest poverty rates in the country, and 71 percent of children in poverty in 2019 were children of color." I would be naive to think that this number was sheer coincidence. It isn't. Instead, I believe that it's part of a well-oiled system of oppression that helps to perpetuate generational trauma.

COVID-19 not only exposed the vast wealth gap between the rich and poor, but it also brought to light what's possible when lawmakers intentionally build a safety net system to lift children out of poverty. The Biden Administration delivered in a huge way by putting cash in the hands of working families. Consequently, according to the US Census, "child poverty, calculated by the Supplemental Poverty Measure (SPM), fell to its lowest recorded level in 2021, declining 46 percent from 9.7 percent in 2020 to 5.2 percent in 2021." But why did it take a catastrophic pandemic that killed thousands and thousands of Americans to do what's morally right? Sadly, with the expiration of the child tax credit, 5.2 million children have been plunged right back into poverty, going to bed without a morsel of food in their hungry bellies.

So, what can educators do to address child poverty? First, take a step back from our assumptions about students based on the way children look or act, especially if they are children of color. For example, take Tom: he wore the same clothes every day, and they were usually dirty; he needed a haircut, his overall appearance was unkempt, and a bad, lingering odor surrounded him. Kids avoided or made fun of him, which caused him to lash out. But he wasn't wearing those dirty clothes because he wanted to. He didn't have any other choice. With permission from his guardian, I took him shopping for new clothes and got him a haircut—the humongous smile on his face as he looked at himself in the mirror all cleaned up just filled me up. I also began helping him wash his clothes at the homeless shelter that adjoined the school.

It didn't take long for Tom's behavior to make a 180-degree change. He graduated high school, and as he walked across the stage, I cried like he was my own. Tom was the first in his family to graduate high school and is doing well today, and all it took was for me to set aside any assumptions and offer a child in need a little bit of care. If you're reading this book, I would encourage you to make a personal commitment to helping a young person escape the harmful grip of poverty. I believe you will.

Housing and Homelessness are Policy Decisions

While educators may have some understanding of how ACEs affect children in school, I doubt that many teachers plan their lessons thinking about the impact of students' zip codes. While zip codes shouldn't matter in terms of opportunities, they do, and the implications are startling.

One such implication is the issue of homelessness, which casts a pervasive shadow over our society. One in thirty youths ages 13–17 will experience homelessness each year. But why are kids experiencing homelessness? The Voices of Youth Court reported that, while youth across all backgrounds and upbringings can become homeless, certain demographics are more susceptible. People of color, people who identify as LGBTQ+, and young parents disproportionately experience youth homelessness at higher rates. Native American youth have more than double the risk of experiencing homelessness compared to other youth. LGBTQ+ youth experience a 120 percent higher risk of becoming homeless after coming out to their families. Additionally, a person's identity can intersect with multiple demographic categories and put them at an even higher risk of homelessness.

To explain this, let's take a walk back into the history which is all too relevant today. The devaluation of Black lives in our nation's past demanded an antidote, but it was President Lyndon Johnson's (adored by some, despised by others) profound insight that led to the protective embrace of Black families through the enactment of the Civil Rights Act of 1964. In a concerted effort to fortify this defense, President Johnson further solidified this commitment on April 11, 1968, when he extended the 1964 predecessor with the Civil Rights Act of 1968. This transformative piece of legislation amplified and fortified its mandates by explicitly barring discrimination in the spheres of housing sales, rentals, and financing based on race, religion, national origin, gender, and, in subsequent amendments, disability and family status. This legislative masterpiece became synonymous with fairness and equity. Recognized as the Fair Housing Act of 1968, Title VIII of this seminal act stood as a resolute step toward dismantling the walls erected by systemic racism.

Despite the strides made to protect Black families from discrimination, racist policies have managed to persist, infiltrating contemporary housing regulations and perpetuating the distressing cycle of segregation that continues to fracture our communities and leave children and families in the cold. This practice, called "redlining," placed parameters on housing appraisals and used color-coded maps to rank neighborhoods based on the "riskiness" of their investment. This redlining, of course, decreased the value of those ranked as the riskiest. Not surprisingly, the "risky" areas were those where Black residents lived. If you are interested in learning more about this history and its continued legacy, *The Color of Law* by Richard Rothstein provides a detailed investigation.

On top of redlining, gentrification is a huge issue for people of color and the poor. This term, coined by sociologist Ruth Glass in the 1960s, is used to describe the phenomenon of an influx of affluent and usually white residents moving to lower-income areas that historically and culturally are communities of color. While it's a nuanced idea whose origins cannot be described simply, the effect is quite simple. People of color are pushed out of their homes and out of their neighborhoods as rents and property taxes rise and the power dynamics shift.

The cumulative impact of these factors reverberates as trauma engenders toxic stress and generates an unrelenting backdrop of adversity that uniquely targets our children. It's a grievous testament that some of these repercussions spiral beyond mere homelessness, spurring transient lifestyles that force children to navigate multiple school districts within the span of a single year.

In addition, the Substance Abuse and Mental Health Services Administration (SAMHSA) noted that "the majority of youth on the street, however, have decided that the challenges and dangers of living in a street environment are preferable to continuing the life they experienced at home, in foster care, or in a group home." This is telling. Children are not on the streets because they want to be. They are there because they often don't have a safe place to call home, and they don't trust government support organizations to properly care for them. It's my profound belief that housing is a basic human right; everyone should have access to housing, and no one should be sleeping outdoors in the harsh elements. However, if the institutions tasked with helping homeless individuals have a long history of traumatizing them, then we are perpetuating generational trauma and harm.

Let's consider Ayun, a cheerful student in the tenth grade. Ayun was homeless and had been couch surfing for several months. The school knew it, the teachers knew it, but they did little or nothing to really help this child. Yet, they still worried about his attendance, grades, and performance on standardized tests. This child couldn't worry about grades—he was worried about where he would sleep, what he would eat, and if he would be physically or sexually abused while sleeping in cars, couch surfing, or spending the night in a shelter. In situations like Ayun's, unless the basic need of safety is adequately responded to, teachers can teach until the cows come home but not much learning will actually be happening. We must recognize that the negative effects of homelessness extend far beyond not having a place to sleep, and then respond accordingly.

As a nation, it's imperative that we confront and embark on the arduous journey of healing the breach engendered by racialized housing policies that were systematically designed to segregate Black individuals from their white counterparts, driven by the toxic forces of white supremacy and the egregious notion of Black inferiority.

It's my firm belief that true anti-racism, allyship, and the pursuit of justice entail an understanding of the interconnectedness between ACEs and the systemic and racialized housing policies that continue to have a profound and lasting impact on Black, Latine, and other children of color. Something that made a huge difference in helping children who were experiencing homelessness was becoming familiar with community wraparound services. I'm lucky to have learned about these services early on when I worked as an intake-outreach coordinator, providing direct services such as food, clothing, and GED and ESL services, along with indirect services such as referrals to other social or government agencies. This role connected me to the many social services agencies in the community. These established and invaluable resources have now become part of my connections, and I'm able to connect students to needed services. Here's an example of how that can work.

One day during lunch period, I was ambling up the staircase when a voice called, "Miss, Miss." I turned around quickly. It was Alexis, a quiet, well-behaved, goal-oriented twelfth-grader. "Miss, I'm homeless." I leaned closer to her and asked, "What do you mean?" What a ridiculous question to ask.

"My dad and I are homeless, Miss, and we're sleeping in a car." She had a smile on her face, but her eyes were filled with sadness. For a moment, I wanted to hug her and just break down. I knew that I couldn't. I had to be the adult; I had to be the strong one.

As she continued sharing her story, I made sure I wasn't interrupting. I knew she wanted to talk, and I wanted her to know that I was present. When children open up to me, I always listen attentively and approach their stories of crisis thoughtfully and with genuine compassion. Then, I always redirect children to avenues of care and support, such as with school counselors or student support services, when I'm not able to help directly.

None of us can singlehandedly solve all the problems that the students sitting before us come to class with. The most we can do is try. At first, I was floored by how seemingly happy, strong, beautiful, and tenacious Alexis was. She was in her senior year and was liked by all of her teachers and classmates. Alexis was always on the move, working hard to get all her credits so she could break the generational curse and become the first person in her family to finish high school and go off to college.

"Is there any way that you can help me?" she asked me. I immediately alerted the school counseling services as to what was going on. In addition to getting Alexis support at school, I also reached out to a respected social service agency, which provided $250 in grocery shopping cards and referrals to nonprofits supporting people experiencing homelessness. Thankfully, Alexis and her father got into emergency housing. Taking swift action meant we could alleviate a significant portion of the stressors that she was facing. As a result of this proactive approach, her attendance improved, as well as her grades. She became more joyful in school and was noticeably happier.

She graduated from high school and was accepted to a local college. Being aware of all the available resources in the community means you or other members of staff can make connections quickly and get children like Alexis back to what's important: building their futures.

Environmental Racism is a Policy Decision

Another implication of unfair housing policy is its impact on the health of residents. In my first year in the Rhode Island General Assembly, I got a call from an irate neighbor about a transfer station going up in the north end of my district. I wasn't sure what that meant, but a quick Google search later, I realized "transfer station" was a fancy name for a garbage dump. I was livid at the thought of a garbage dump within walking distance from E-Cubed Academy, the high school where I taught. The transfer station would also be in the North End of Providence, which is home to many older residents, many of whom have compromised immune systems. I quickly put on my organizing hat, coordinating efforts in the community alongside local businesses that would be impacted negatively by such a facility. Before long, we were able to thwart the transfer station from coming to our neighborhood.

This experience is one many lower-income neighborhoods must face, and when city boards approve hazardous facilities to operate in these neighborhoods, it's the young and infirm who suffer most. Children who live in impoverished neighborhoods confront the dire consequences of this environmental racism, leading to elevated incidences of asthma and other respiratory illnesses. Housing students in sub-standard school buildings also results from a system that perpetuates the inequity inherent in redlining. For example, respiratory issues were rampant at one of my schools; teachers and children got so sick from poor and inadequate ventilation that our teachers' union filed grievances on our behalf. It wasn't just for us; it was for the students and every single person who was in that building daily. Rhode Island is notorious for substandard school buildings, and the state was ranked in the top ten for asthma rates in the United States. In a report funded by a grant from the Environmental Agency and published in an online article by ecoRI News, the suggestion was made that in some of the poorest cities in the state, 10.9 percent of the population suffered from a respiratory condition. Rhode Island, the article continued, "has the ninth highest rate of asthma in the country." To address the issue of sub-standard school buildings, over the last few years the government has been making an effort to improve or build new schools; these couldn't come soon enough.

After reading the report on the percentage of people with asthma in my home state, a zillion thoughts flooded through my mind, triggering an eruption of emotions. Where I grew up in Bull Bay, it was neither rural nor urban. It was both. My neighborhood had factories making hosiery, sheet metal, electrical lighting, hair processing cream, and other products. Of course, the factories rarely hired locals. But what they did was spew toxins into our neighborhood. Rhode Island is grappling with similar ills, yet these types of environmental racism and the systemic devaluing of impoverished people is not a local problem. It's a pervasive global predicament that requires and demands immediate climate action.

Another fight that I, along with members of my community, waged was to resist wealthy corporations from putting a liquefied natural gas (LNG) plant on the south side of Providence. South Providence is a densely populated area of the city where some of our poorest children and their families live and attend run-down schools. As a public-school teacher, as well as a former member of the Rhode Island General Assembly representing my students and families, I was a strong voice advocating for clean air for students. In my 2018 testimony to the Coastal Resources Management Council, the agency responsible for preserving, developing, and restoring coastal resources in Rhode Island, I was quoted as saying, "This matter before you today will adversely affect my neighbors in an already compromised neighborhood. I know this is a form of environmental injustice and environmental racism. By wanting to build the LNG plant, it sends a clear message that National Grid does not care about infants, children, seniors, our poorest and most vulnerable citizens, many of whom are already suffering from compromised immune systems." Those were and still are my exact thoughts on the matter of environmental racism.

Drawing from this distressing situation, I introduced HB-5784: Health and Safety of Pupils. This act would direct the Department of Health to establish a comprehensive inspection and evaluation program assessing air quality in public schools. Unfortunately, no action was taken on this piece of legislation. So, what can teachers, students, and families do? We must continue to raise our voices and engage with our elected officials to demand safer schools. This isn't a choice; it's a moral imperative.

A Teacher Who Looks Like You

I fervently hope that every child in every classroom has a multitude of individuals in their schools that make them feel exceptional. This is especially vital for Black and brown children. These children need an abundance of role models who look like them, share a cultural and linguistic background with them, and resonate with their lived experiences. This is important for many reasons, including that it fosters a sense of belonging, fuels self-confidence, and strengthens connections between students and their learning environment. It also gives them role models of success, showing them that they can grow up and do something important with their lives. The significance of representation cannot be overstated.

In my years of teaching, I have witnessed white teachers blatantly ignore Latine students and newcomers from Africa or other Caribbean countries. I have seen students being dismissed and their contributions to classroom discussions ignored. I have heard teachers say, "Shut up," or worse, "I can't understand your accent," and simply move on to other students, thus minimizing and embarrassing the students. This is traumatizing and rooted in racist attitudes toward Black, brown, and other children of color.

I know how it feels to be in traditionally white spaces where I'm made to feel invisible. It is not a good feeling. I have also been in schools where children of color, kids receiving special education services, kids in wheelchairs, kids in foster care, and poor white children are invisible. By acknowledging and valuing each student and elevating all of their voices, stories, and lived experiences, we support a positive climate and culture while creating agency in the classroom. Therefore, it's important that we hold each other accountable when we witness the marginalization or mistreatment of any child in any classroom.

Though the importance of representation has always been at the forefront of my mind, never was it more visible than after I won my seat to the House of Representatives. After beating out the Democratic incumbent in a campaign that mainly focused on my race and ethnic background, I decided to take a teaching job in my beloved Wanskuck neighborhood, the area I'd lived for twenty-four years. This meant I would have to say goodbye to the tenth-grade students I had at the time.

It was a difficult goodbye and some of the students couldn't hold back tears. I knew that loss, a form of trauma, could bring up difficult feelings for these kids, especially as many of them had experienced losing loved ones to gun violence, the foster system, or the criminal punishment system. Though I was leaving for a good reason and nothing bad was happening to me, the loss still triggered those feelings of brokenness and being left alone.

Two years later, I ran into one of those students, a bright young girl named Euphemia, who was transformed into a powerful and formidable advocate. She was dedicating her evenings to lobbying for clean and safe drinking water. What's also impressive was that Euphemia had taken the State of Rhode Island to court to ensure that civics education became a mandatory core element of the curriculum that would be taught in public schools. Her journey was nothing short of inspiring, a testament to the power of education to shape passionate, empowered citizens.

When Euphemia spotted me, she dashed over, enveloped me with a huge hug, and planted a kiss on my cheek. "Miss, I miss you so much! You were the only teacher who cared, and now we have so many young white teachers. Miss, why did you leave? Why did you leave?" She demanded an answer.

I didn't know what to say and just mumbled that I wanted to live and work in my district, the district I was representing. Though I was so happy to see her and hear all about the important work she was doing, an overwhelming wave of shame showered over me. I'd abandoned this child, abandoned all the children at that school. The thoughts that flooded my mind tormented me.

I hated the fact that Euphemia felt abandoned by me. But it wasn't just her; it was D'zire, Angela, Brian, Karla, Safina, Brayan, Diarra, Nayeli, Edward, and all the other Black and Latine children I'd left behind. A zillion questions raced through my mind. Was I the only teacher in the school who made Euphemia feel special? Could I reverse the decision I'd made?

I found no answer that made sense, so with tears in my eyes, I went to sit in my chair, not as a teacher, not as a legislator, but as a human being filled with the emotions of letting this remarkable child down. In that moment of internal conflict, titles and roles faded into insignificance; what remained was the profound responsibility and a deep heartfelt connection to that young child. I was hard on myself after that conversation. Teaching is a difficult job, and sometimes it feels like we're carrying water in baskets, as my late grandmother Lillian would say. But it's in these pivotal moments that educators must see themselves as human beings and seek grace wherever it may be found, in themselves or in the world.

What helped me was opening my journal and reading the going away messages that those kids penned for me. Reading their messages filled me with hope. I earnestly hope that they, like Euphemia, are out there in the world making bold moves to change not only the trajectory of their own lives but also the lives of their families as well.

Diversity is not simply about the color of our skin. Diversity involves all of us seeing each other and acknowledging the gifts and talents that we all have to offer. For kids who experience trauma in their own homes, communities, or group homes, being shut down by grown-ups is often a part of their existence. They don't need more of it at school. One way to dismantle this is by practicing inclusivity and recognizing every single voice in your classroom. Morning and afternoon check-ins are a good way to get even the quietest kids out of their shells. These conversations are low-key and don't incorporate any structured kind of learning. Instead, kids are encouraged to share simple and light conversation. For example, after a quick movement break where all the students dance, I might ask kids to share about their favorite fruits and why they like them. Morning meetings set the tone for the entire day.

Time magazine stated that "slightly more than 20% of public-school teachers—who include those at charter schools—in the U.S. identify as people of color, compared with more than half of students. Only 7% of teachers identify as Black." But their research also showed that "students of color perform better academically, and are more likely to stay in school, when they are exposed to teachers of their race or ethnicity. White students benefit too."

So why aren't there more teachers of color? There is a myriad of reasons for this, including low pay—especially as teachers of color are more likely to teach at less affluent schools—burnout from experiencing microaggressions or overt racism, trying to navigate cultural incompetence from white colleagues and administrators, and more. Oftentimes, it's the Black teacher, Latine teacher, or other teacher of color who has to speak up on issues of race that everyone else is ignoring. Many times, the teacher of color is the only one advocating for anti-racist curricula or opposing book bans. Some schools, especially in the wake of the 2020 Black Lives Matter resurgence, have tried to focus more attention on issues of race. But in doing so, they often lean too heavily on teachers of color, expecting them to spend extra time and energy, without any extra compensation, being the advocate and educator for the rest of the team. This is exhausting. School districts should not only continue the conversation of teacher retention but also commit to actionable steps to protect the mental and physical health of Black teachers and teachers of color. In doing so, school systems will be created where all teachers, along with their students, are able to thrive.

Helpful Hints from Teachers

- *Leave your ego at the door;* teaching is not about you.

- *Look around at the kids in your classroom.* If they differ from you in terms of race, gender, ability, or so on, find a book or other resource to understand them better.

- *Allow yourself to make mistakes.* When you do, own them and learn from them. This shows your students that you're human—just like them. They will see that, if their teacher can make mistakes, then they can too.

- *Make friends with the school secretary and the stockroom clerk*—they run the school!

- *Stay up to date on new research and best practices in education.* As the demographics of our nation changes, so will best classroom practices. Make sure you are on the cutting edge!

- *Do your best to remain calm, use soft tones, and show profound empathy.*

CHAPTER 4

SECONDARY TRAUMA

JASON WAS A twenty-two-year-old white male teacher living in the suburbs when he took a teaching job in a part of an urban city known for its high rates of crime and violence. He describes Faith High School as where he "cut his teeth in teaching."

After earning his bachelor's in Secondary Education, Jason was overly anxious to put all he knew into his budding career as a teacher. Unfortunately, he was unprepared for the traumatic stories he was hearing. He painstakingly recalls a young girl telling him that she was sexually abused by her own father. When she told her mother and the rest of the family, they said there was no validity to her story, and that if she told anyone, she would destroy the family as her father was the main breadwinner. Jason recalled that this child was now trusting him, another man, her teacher, with her story. Decades later, he still admires her courage and hopes that she's alright, but at the time, he had a hard time processing the girl's trauma. Her story and the stories of other kids sitting in front of him kept him up all night; he could barely eat, couldn't concentrate, and he found himself in a state of emotional shock.

He started reliving some of his own unresolved trauma.

This is because Jason has no training in trauma education, so he didn't know how it impacted a child's brain or what to do with the horrific stories he was hearing. He remembers asking the student who told him of the abuse what she wanted him to do. The only thing that he knew from his college training was that he had a duty to report it. He immediately did. He also knew that he should provide an empathetic ear. Shocked, angered, and feeling helpless, he turned to a few older women in his building who supported him emotionally and guided him. He fondly refers to them as his mentors. However, Jason, like many other teachers, hasn't seen a mental health counselor, though he continues to hear horrific stories from his students. He merely hopes that time will heal him. He doesn't realize he's suffering from "secondary trauma."

"Secondary trauma" is the emotional distress that occurs when hearing about the trauma that others have experienced. It's a toxic force that infiltrates our bodily systems and harms us both mentally and physically. Basically, this kind of trauma transmits its impact indirectly to unsuspecting individuals through bearing witness to the traumatic narratives of others. Secondary trauma mirrors the symptoms of PTSD, including anxiety and depression, inadequate sleep, irritability, exhaustion, anger, despair, a sense of hopelessness, pervasive sadness, diminished interest in sex or intimacy, and loss of appetite.

Experiencing too much secondary trauma without any recourse can lead to "compassion fatigue," which, according to the Administration for Children and Families, "is associated with a sense of confusion, helplessness, and a greater sense of isolation from supporters than is seen with burnout." Secondary trauma can—and should—be treated through a combination of counseling, therapy, and/or medication, as postulated by an online article captioned: "Secondary Traumatic Stress." For all of us experiencing symptoms of secondary trauma, it therefore behooves us to seek competent care in a timely manner.

In this chapter, I will take a look at the secondary trauma that affects children as well as educators to offer a full picture of the stressors that we are trying to alleviate.

Secondary Trauma and Students

As discussed in Chapter 1, kids are under all kinds of stressors. They experience first-hand trauma such as abuse or hunger, but many also experience secondary trauma through things like hearing their parents fighting, seeing domestic violence, or witnessing people getting shot. These kinds of trauma don't happen directly to them, but they still feel the effects that can have long-lasting negative repercussions on their mental health and physical well-being.

As discussed in previous chapters, the COVID-19 pandemic exacerbated the challenges faced by all children. Not only did the pandemic increase poverty, homelessness, and stress, but it was also a huge source of secondary trauma that many are still living with. Further, it's worth noting that the impacts were often more severe for children of color and those living in poverty. If students were living in an unsafe space where they were witnessing the trauma of their parents, siblings, or neighbors, the pandemic forced them to be in that space all the time. There was no escape to school or community centers. Although that time of isolation has ended, the scars of what many witnessed still remain, and children continue to go home to see more trauma at the end of the night.

For many children, especially those living traumatic lives, school is their cocoon, their shelter, and their safe zone. For some, it's the only place they feel safe enough to sleep or the only place where they can get a hot meal. School is where many are able to be kids. I remember a story told to me by another teacher about a young boy crying at the end of the school day. The other students were heading home, but he had "lost" his shoes. The teacher was searching frantically for them. After what seemed like forever, they finally located the shoes. Later, the teacher found out that it was the child who had intentionally hidden his own shoes because he didn't want to go home. The teacher was able to connect the boy with a school psychologist, but what was evident was that, at school, he felt a sense of belonging, felt loved, and wanted to stay there.

School should be a safe space for children. A place to heal from the trauma they are experiencing or seeing, and a place where they learn that they can succeed. As educators, we must take into account that even children who come to school in clean new clothes and get fed square meals at home may be experiencing secondary trauma. Those traumatic events may be a reason why students are acting out, emotionally numb, or not doing well academically. In instances where teachers aren't sure, they should err on the side of caution and refer to the school's social work team.

Secondary Trauma and Teachers

Among those who are most vulnerable to this reverberation are our dedicated first responders. This group comprises doctors, nurses, police officers, social workers, psychologists, behavior interventionists, school counselors, and other mental health professionals who are on the front line of human suffering. Yet, in the wake of the pandemic, teachers and paraprofessionals have also found themselves thrust into a thankless role, further underscoring the paramount importance of our steadfast commitment to nurturing and safeguarding the health and well-being of students.

I fully acknowledge how burdensome and overwhelming the job of a teacher can be. I know from first-hand experience how difficult it is to prioritize our own mental and physical health when we are so focused on getting help for our students. However, we must. Just like the flight attendant instructs us to put our own oxygen mask on first before attempting to help others in an emergency, we must make our own mental health care and well-being a priority.

Oftentimes, educators and paraprofessionals mask their feelings, fearing vulnerability or being construed as weak, ineffective, or incompetent. However, you're not alone in feeling burned out, overly stressed, emotionally numb, or any other type of way. It means you're human and what you may be experiencing is secondary trauma. An online article published by the Association for Supervision and Curriculum Development (ASCD) entitled "The Trauma Transmission from Students to Teachers" (Gross, 2020) explains that "trauma's psychological transmission to teachers can manifest itself in several ways, including symptomology that resembles burnout and through vicarious trauma, which threatens our core values and capacity to work effectively."

With plates so full and schools not always offering needed support, teachers may not even be aware of what's occurring in their own bodies because this secondary trauma isn't always easily identified. Teachers are too busy planning lessons, grading, coaching, supervising extracurricular activities, spending one-on-one time with students, and so many other tasks that they don't leave any time for themselves. This oversight can be costly and is certainly part of the reason why many great and compassionate teachers leave the profession. What doesn't help is the way schools are structured to mirror businesses, with profit being the only thing that appears to matter. When money supersedes introspection, more stress is placed on the entire school community and everyone is left looking over their shoulders, worried that their work won't be enough. In this climate, it becomes easy to neglect the self-awareness necessary to take care of themselves. Fostering a culture open to dialogue is paramount to safeguarding the mental and physical health of educators, students, and the entire school community.

Not all teachers "just want to teach" the curriculum. Some of us are empaths. We carry the stories of our students in our minds, bodies, and souls. Our students spend most of their waking hours with us, upward of six or seven hours per day. Families may not even know this, but once they trust us, kids tell their teachers almost everything. We know most everything that happens in the home. It feels wonderful when a student trusts you enough to share their hardships and you can get help for them. But being the receptacle of all that pain and suffering takes a toll.

There have been moments as a teacher that I've felt alone, help-less, and sad. I remember one point when I was having constant and terrible headaches and losing sleep. Although my personal life was filled with love, I laid down in my bed every night feeling exhausted. It was as if I was experiencing a deep sense of hopeless-ness. I felt terrible that I was never in the right head space to enjoy time with my family—I was always stuck on a student's story, wondering if one had dinner or worrying that another wouldn't have a bed to sleep in.

By the time I realized I was suffering from secondary trauma, it was eroding my inner joy, something that I have always prided myself on. I knew I couldn't go on like this and continue to serve my kids to the best of my abilities. Something had to change. It's in these moments that we must recognize who we are and prioritize our own health and well-being. By nurturing ourselves, we will be better able to champion and advocate for the needs of the students entrusted to our care.

One of the tools that I carry in my self-care kit is a pocket journal. It has helped me for as long as I can remember. I was an inquisitive child who needed more answers than my parents could or wanted to give, and I always found solace in writing. Over the years, I have journaled to help heal myself as well as to make sense of the world. When I was going through this dark time, I realized that I hadn't journaled in a while; I was letting all those sad and horrific stories pile up inside of me. I was carrying them around in my heart, in my body, and in my soul, and they were weighing me down.

So, I started journaling each night before bed, just letting the stories flow out of me and onto the pages of my journal. I let loose the feelings, emotions, and anger I kept bottled up to remain calm and protective of the children. One of the first entries was about a mother and her daughter who had become homeless because she was having trouble making rent.

I didn't sleep well last night. I tossed and turned all night thinking of her. I kept seeing her beautiful face, her long blond hair, streaked with tinges of gray; it was beautiful. She had a gentle smile as she shared her story. Her eyes were pale, sad, and filled with pain. I didn't ask her how old or how young she was. I suspect she may be in her late forties, early fifties. She began to recall her story of not knowing how she and her daughter became homeless. It just happened, she said, while she was working full time and making $11.50 an hour.

"I'm a poor woman," she said. "I'm a working mom, but I am struggling every day to keep the roof over my head and to make ends meet, and it doesn't matter what I do, I just can't catch up."

I moved closer to her and held her hands. "I am so sorry that you're going through this. I want you to know that as long as God gives me breath, I will never stop my fight for $15 an hour. I am so, so sorry for what you're going through." As I walked away, a million tears rolled down my cheeks and I carried this mom in my heart.

Of course, writing this journal entry didn't solve that mother's problem. It didn't get the minimum wage increase I'd been fighting for. However, it allowed me to sleep that night and feel more like myself in the morning. Feeling refreshed, with a clearer mind and lighter spirit, I was able to refocus my efforts and continue working toward my goal of a $15 minimum wage.

This is the thing about secondary trauma. Teachers, thankfully, may not be suffering from desperately low wages, but policy decisions that perpetuate poverty still impact them. As they care for their students and their students' families, teachers feel residual stress from hearing their students' stories, addressing their students' trauma response behaviors, or attempting to compensate for their students' systematic learning deficits. To address this specific cause of secondary stress, one must fight for policy change. This is why raising the minimum wage has been a battle of mine, one of my top three priorities, since I was first elected. I'm happy to report that in 2024, legislation was passed to bump the minimum wage up to $14 per hour (from $13 in 2023). That same legislation will continue a gradual increase to $15 per hour in 2025. There's much more to keep fighting for, but this win puts us on the path toward breaking the cycle of poverty that causes both direct and secondary stress in our schools. It's my hope that one day, working families and the students I teach who sadly have to skip school to go to work will realize the dream of being paid what they are worth—a dignified wage and a less traumatic life. Until that time comes, I will keep fighting for all of us.

Creating a Space for Healing and Growth

In order to defend against secondary trauma, it's important for teachers to practice self-care, self-compassion, and self-preservation. As educators, we're not inanimate objects devoid of emotions.

We have feelings, thoughts, and emotions. We empathize, internalize, and absorb the pain of others, allowing it to seep deep inside our bodily systems. But the pain of others doesn't have to be a death sentence for us. It's possible to navigate and experience pain and joy simultaneously.

I've candidly discussed the stress that has accompanied my life both inside and outside the classroom. Juggling the multiple roles of being a wife, mother, grandmother, sister, teacher, and caregiver is no small feat, but I'm doing it the best way I know. The truth is that these roles don't magically disappear when I'm at school, but I've learned to integrate them in ways that augment my work as a teacher.

I often think of my own mother, who came at life's challenges with a ferocious confidence. She wasn't a teacher—she didn't finish primary school, let alone attend college—but she was strong in the moments that she needed to be, always pushing against the winds of poverty. Mom always had a recipe to make things work. In my moments of despair, in those moments where I feel stressed, I channel her quiet strength and tenacity. They keep me going.

There's an old adage, "You can't pour from an empty cup." It's cliché because it's true! We cannot support our children if we have no reservoir of self-care. Sadie, an experienced teacher in a huge public high school, told me that, for her, the cup doesn't even exist anymore. Recognizing her own mental health state, she says her cup is broken. The way she tries hard to love and care for herself now is by doing Google searches and trying to find self-care approaches. Unfortunately, Sadie ends up doing one internet search after the other. It's my hope that she finds help in this book. Standing united in our quest to educate our children doesn't mean we neglect our own lives. If we can't adequately care for ourselves and compassionately address our own trauma, then we may inflict more on our students. In the spirit of love and trauma-informed education, teachers and other professionals helping traumatized children must do everything to maintain and protect their mental health.

Guarding your own health and well-being is not a selfish act—it's self-preservation. In Part Three, I'll delve more deeply into self-care practices and ideas. Remember always that, as an educator, you're a beacon of light to others, and just as we extend that light to guide our students, we must also allow that same light to illuminate our own path. By nurturing our own souls, we amplify the capacity to lift others.

Teaching is a backbreaking, emotionally draining endeavor. Teaching cannot just be a profession; it's a mission, a passion. Educators also often wear many hats, being more than just the person conveying the facts needed to pass the tests. This requires a lot of effort. Without support, we're sure to buckle under the weight of it all.

Now that I've offered an outline of the issues facing students and educators, in Part Two we'll take a look at the systemic change that I know is the solution: trauma-informed practices and schools.

Helpful Hints from Teachers

- *Think of education as a three-legged stool:* it cannot stand if one of its legs is broken.

- *Collaborate with your peers,* including related service providers and paraprofessionals. Don't try to do it all by yourself. Provide continuous feedback to all stakeholders (other teachers, parents, administration, community organizations, and others).

- *Seek out and find a mentor in or out of your school.* These are others who understand what you're going through and can provide you tips or help you share the weight of your burden.

- *Add a pocket journal to your self-care kit.* The process of writing is really helpful in releasing stress and tension from your body.

- *If you're going through tumultuous times, seek out professional help.* I cannot stress this enough. If you feel homicidal or suicidal, call 988. There are mental health counselors waiting on the other end of the line to help you right away.

PART TWO

A TRAUMA-INFORMED WAY OF LIFE

CHAPTER 5

TRAUMA-INFORMED PRACTICES AT SCHOOL

MS. KETTLE IS A beacon of relentless strength and compassion. She once told me a tragic and heart-wrenching account of how one of her students went home in the midst of the pandemic to find her mom's lifeless body, dead from an overdose of drugs. This young student was suddenly thrust into the predicament of having to take care of herself while processing the tragedy. With this unexpected event, she missed about three weeks of school. Understandably, she struggled to stay focused in class.

Ms. Kettle collaborated with the guidance counselor and classroom teachers to significantly reduce the student's workload, lightening her academic burden so she could fully focus on her emotional well-being. This is the core of trauma-informed practices, which is what we'll be exploring in this chapter. We all want children to succeed, get good grades, graduate, and do amazing things in their lives, but how we help them achieve those goals requires looking at them as a whole person.

My goal for this chapter is to define Social-Emotional Learning and trauma-informed practices as well as offer real-life examples of how to incorporate this type of teaching into every school day. I also offer a broader view of what changes need to be made to ensure that we have schools operate in trauma-informed and trauma-aware ways on every level.

Social-Emotional Learning

Amidst the ongoing shortage of teachers, most days I find myself playing dual roles in the classroom: general education teacher, teacher assistant, and special education teacher. Within minutes of beginning my fourth period lesson in a class where the general education teacher had been out on medical leave for well over a month, Kalee, a beautiful girl with rainbow-colored hair, blurted out from the back, "What the f*ck you're trying to do? You're not even the real teacher."

She became more and more disruptive as I explained that I was filling in to support the class while her teacher was away. I moved closer to her to calm her down, but she got more agitated as I approached, saying, "Get away from me."

Another girl beside her turned to her and said, "You don't even know who she is? Google her!"

Kalee took her phone out and Googled my name. With a startled look, she peered up at me and asked, "Why are you even here?"

"I'm here for you, Kalee. That's why I'm here." Kalee and I looked at each other and gave a synchronized smile. Without another word, she opened her novel, ready to read.

After decades spent in the classroom, I've concluded that children don't act out with the deliberate intention to cause trouble. In the case of Kalee, I don't for one minute believe that her outburst was because she wanted me to be angry or because she wanted to make my day miserable. Instead, she was simply responding to the feelings of abandonment she had with the loss of the teacher she had come to care about. Kalee, like many other students, reacted to complex triggers of underlying trauma and acted out with impulses that she herself might not be able to identify, never mind address.

For both first-year teachers or even seasoned professionals faced with dysregulated behaviors in children, the first step is engaging in a non-confrontational manner. To be non-confrontational may mean simply ignoring the outburst as long as you have assessed the situation and determined that no one is at risk of getting hurt. In that particular scenario, I knew instantaneously that engaging in a battle of words with Kalee would never yield a positive outcome, so why bother? Plus, my knowledge of trauma and how it manifests itself continues to guide my interactions.

It's important to note that the objective is not to force compliance from the children but rather to foster relationships where time spent in the classroom is productive for both teacher and learner. So, how can we share power in the classroom so everyone wins? Firstly, I think that educators should consider dropping the idea of power altogether. Feeling that you own all the power in the classroom sets up barriers and isn't conducive to teaching and learning. Classrooms must be places of joyful resilience, exploration, and learning, not places where power is exerted. The student who prompted Kalee to "Google" me demonstrated shared power. It was that child's efforts to maintain a respectful class environment that helped Kalee understand that she needed to trust me as another teacher.

According to the Collaborative for Academic, Social, and Emotional Learning (CASEL), Social-Emotional Learning (SEL) is "the process through which all young people and adults acquire and apply the knowledge, skills, and attitudes to develop healthy identities, manage emotions and achieve personal and collective goals, feel and show empathy for others, establish and maintain supportive relationships, and make responsible and caring decisions." In short, employing SEL means that schools are responsible for teaching students to self-regulate in a manner where they can take charge of their own reactions and their own learning.

Let's explore this scenario: Imagine you rescued a puppy from the animal shelter. The puppy has endured hardships and experienced abuse, hunger, and fear while living as a stray. Upon arriving at your home, the puppy promptly destroys the couch and pees all over the house. You may wonder, "Why is he or she acting out!?" While it could be easy to get mad at the puppy to whom you've only given love, food, and nice toys, you have a few other options. You can take the puppy back to the shelter, you can "discipline" him or her, send the pup to therapy care, or you can research how to provide her care and well-being through gentle and consistent training. No matter the choice, you must realize that the puppy has been through a lot, is scared, and is acting out because a puppy can't communicate its fears or understand the expectations of her new environment. She must learn.

Therefore, you choose patience, getting the puppy some personalized training, playing calming music, and making sure you feed and walk the animal on a regular and predictable schedule. You are also providing training in how to react to other humans, how to wait patiently for dinner or play, and how to earn treats. What you are doing is providing a loving and supportive environment in which your puppy can learn that it's safe and that it's okay to just be a happy puppy. By doing so, you are also providing your pet with behavioral tools to help regulate reactions.

Children aren't puppies, but, like all beings, our students require love, patience, and care to flourish and thrive. They also need direct instruction on how to interact with others and how to express themselves when they are upset. We must be willing to create a supportive and trusting school community rich in pedagogy and high standards, but those standards must not harm kids in any way. At its core, schools should be centers of learning, supporting children who have been through so much. Borrowing the title of one my favorite poets, Tupac Shakur, just like "The Rose That Grew from Concrete," your students can and will thrive given the right people and the right support in our schools.

As I think of Social-Emotional Learning and try to process the implications in my own classroom, I think of how my co-workers and I can be deliberate in helping kids develop self and social awareness, self-control, self-management, and relationship skills. I think of how, as educators, we can model those same behaviors that are expected of our students as they interact with their peers in their school or broader community.

We must find new ways to create safe spaces whereby kids get to explore and connect to themselves, others, and their emotions in new ways. To model this, one of my co-teachers, Steph, and I usually begin the day with activities that help kids regulate their thoughts and emotions while actively interacting with classmates. Sometimes the activity may be writing or speaking about something or someone that they are grateful for. Other times it's beginning the class with beautiful music and encouraging dancing. Sometimes we do deep breathing, helping kids to be still and peaceful as they embark on the new school day. They might not learn facts to help them pass the class, but they are developing skills that they will take with them into adulthood.

Social-Emotional Learning is not just about understanding or teaching a curriculum. It's about building resilient and supportive human beings—something that I'd consider more important than any good grade. Reframing the mindset to intentionally focus on Social-Emotional Learning is a pathway to achieving social, behavioral, and academic outcomes. My school district, along with many others around the country, has incorporated CASEL's nationally recognized standards and skills in K-12 classrooms: self-awareness, self-management, social awareness, relationship skills, and decision-making. I'm appreciative of this path in helping kids thrive.

When you have an understanding of each student as a child, incorporating SEL into your lessons just makes sense. Please note that SEL is not a subject that you teach; it's infused in every aspect of your school day.

What are Trauma-Informed Practices?

Trauma-informed practices are a dynamic process that emerges when educators, school districts, paraprofessionals, and related service providers approach their roles with a deep awareness and understanding of ACEs and the profound impact that they have on the architecture of children's brains. Embedding trauma-informed practices within the educational framework requires an SEL curriculum rooted in research and a foundation of trust, empathy, and compassion while consistently utilizing an equity lens. It means embedding trauma-informed practices every day, embracing the whole child, employing a collaborative approach, utilizing restorative justice, acknowledging racial and social inequality, and adopting a growth mentality.

First, trauma-informed practices cannot be used in a single area of the curriculum. I've heard educators say, "It's time to teach SEL, so let me include trauma-informed practices in Advisory." But these practices cannot be divorced from the rest of the day; they must be used consistently. The essence of trauma-informed practices lies in its ongoing nature, prioritizing healing, growth, and resilience over punishment. Classrooms that embody these practices move from a rigid format and procedures to one that embraces adaptability and flexibility.

This might look like a pause halfway through your instruction for a brain break, or it may mean doing a hands-on project to break up a day full of computer time. I've found that engagement and retention of lessons are positively impacted by this style of flexible learning. As educators, we must be flexible so that we're able to bend and not break. Classrooms where there is flexibility and adaptability are spaces where every member of the education team integrates SEL, not only in pedagogy but in all aspects of school activities. I highly recommend this approach as it fosters the holistic development of each child.

Secondly, trauma-informed practices go well beyond the perspective of just fixing children. Children who have had or are experiencing significant challenges in their lives are not damaged or broken. Shifting mindsets and teaching from a place of equity and compassion must always be our compass and guide. As educators and paraprofessionals, we must recognize the inherent wholeness, beauty, and resilience within each child, while acknowledging the horrors, complex trauma, and toxic stress that some face. Taking a holistic approach means embracing the responsibility to care for these children who have witnessed and endured unimaginable difficulties and still get up each morning to come to school. Let us begin to see kids for exactly who they are: strong, beautiful, creative, funny, and most of all, resilient.

In addition, trauma-informed schools are those that cultivate a school culture steeped in love, compassion, and empathy. This practice applies to the teachers, but just as importantly to all the other adults, whether they be nurses, bus drivers, or administrators. Together, we must commit to a collaborative approach, creating a web of communication and support. Trauma-informed schools that employ collaboration are places where parents, guardians, and caregivers are welcomed, valued, engaged, and feel like they have a stake in their child's education. As educators, we must all do a better job at building strong bonds and relationships to drive our instruction. Of course, every classroom is different and there are no prescribed formulas for this, but we must find pathways to building tolerance, empathy, love, and compassion. Cultivating stronger bonds and connections with students, support and administrative staff, and parents means acknowledging the diverse needs and experiences of the community, while facilitating growth and well-being.

Stepping out of our comfort zone and interacting with others we don't know can be challenging. It's important to recognize that this isn't always easy for some students, so they especially need models of relationship builders. With all that classroom teachers, paraprofessionals, administrators, and other related service providers have to do in the course of their day, it's hard to be excellent at everything. But if we're going to choose just one thing to get better at, make it the student-teacher bond; everything grows from the strength of that relationship. This includes walking down the hallway and being intentional about speaking to the children you see sitting on the stairway or those sauntering in the hallways. As educators, we must commit to speaking to children without just giving them directives. These organic conversations help to build strong bonds for future learning. For real estate agents, it's Location! Location! Location! For us educators, it's Relationships! Relationships! Relationships!

Next, trauma-informed schools use and value restorative justice instead of retaliation or punishment of students. By utilizing a trauma-informed lens, educators possess a greater understanding of how attention-seeking behaviors or what can also be considered disruptive behaviors could be a call for help. For example, Caroline was a student who constantly horsed around and was the self-proclaimed class clown. While her humor was undeniably amusing, it often surfaced at inopportune moments, mostly during direct instruction. After reflecting on, observing, and decoding her behaviors, I figured out that humor was a coping mechanism when the task was too difficult and she was unable to do it independently.

I had known Caroline from a previous class and had a healthy relationship with her. Immediately, I set a time to talk with her. During our meeting, I celebrated how funny she was. I told her that she had a knack for comedy and that I appreciated her talent. I asked her if she noticed that I, too, liked to add a bit of humor in the often-dry classroom. She laughed, and I laughed too. I was transparent with her and told her my observations about why she was disruptive with humor. She acknowledged that I was correct. I told her that while humor and laughter should be in all classrooms, sometimes it could be distracting and could interfere, especially when the teacher was teaching. I also told her that if any task was difficult, I would be willing to assist her and welcomed her to join me once per week for after-school tutoring. She did. Her behavior in class quieted down, and she learned to channel her humor into more appropriate moments.

All of this came about from one simple conversation in which I was intentional about beginning the conversation with acknowledgment and love, focusing on our shared qualities and why I appreciated her as an individual. Then, we were able to have an open conversation about the issue. Finally, I offered specific suggestions for ways to move forward, letting her know that she would have my continued support. This is trauma-informed education at work.

Finally, and unequivocally, let me state that just having an understanding of what ACEs are isn't enough to constitute trauma-informed teaching. Too often, educators believe that getting continuing education credits or just checking off the boxes is enough. That may be enough to satisfy your Board of Education's standards or allow you to put something new on your resume, but it's certainly not enough to help struggling students.

To illustrate, I was once at a training for teachers and overheard two teachers talking. One described the kids in her class as "the worst of the worst." She continued her hurtful conversation by saying the kids were so bad that they just needed to be thrown away. My heart sank. Of course, I kept my mouth shut, but later that day I sought out and had a conversation with the teacher. I commiserated that I understood how difficult our job is and mentioned some trauma-informed practices that had been useful to me. She countered by saying she had taken courses on trauma-informed classrooms. But she was very stuck on how "bad" she perceived her students to be, saying that none of her training had helped her to deal with "those kids." Those kids. Let that sink in. There was an obvious disconnect between what was learned and what was practiced, but I do believe in redemption, so we all learn, grow, and thrive.

I empathized with her, acknowledging her concerns and letting her know that sometimes I, too, found it difficult to put these practices to work. There's no one-size-fits-all trauma-informed approach, and each of us is learning as we go. Being intentional and not giving up on kids is key. She got very emotional and confessed that she was at the end of her rope, feeling overwhelmed and stressed out. She wanted to love her kids again, but she had no bandwidth for it. I knew she was suffering from secondary trauma. At the end of the conversation, I gave her my number, and now she's a part of my circle of teachers who support other teachers.

Gaining knowledge and honing skills through targeted and specialized professional development training or research is only a starting point. It's in the application of these insights and best practices that educators and school staff truly make a difference in helping students thrive.

I love to talk to others, and I'm encouraged by educators at the top of their learning game who are doing everything possible to educate children so they grow and thrive. One such educator is Alex. I sat across from Alex in a small room that serves both as a library and classroom on the third floor of her school. She's been teaching for well over twenty-five years but is still open to learning and growing. With a wealth of teaching knowledge, Alex is quick to admit that she will not pretend to know what it means to be Black or brown, but she sure knows what it means to be poor and white, as she grew up in a rural area of Appalachia.

Alex insists that to be trauma-informed means holding high standards while teaching to the whole child. Her realization of this principle crystallized early on when she taught adjudicated kids in a prison setting. Confronted with kids who carried heavy emotional baggage, Alex realized that the conventional approach to rote learning wouldn't suffice and that students needed many and differentiated levels of support to achieve their learning potential. After reading the works of educator, activist, and author Geoffrey Canada, Alex crafted an "all hands on deck" approach to instruction that places all children, but especially children with the most challenges, at the center of her mission. This is the essence of the trauma-informed approach and growth mindset.

Furthermore, school staff must also commit to racial, educational, and economic equity while embracing a strong intrinsic desire for more personal growth and development. Trauma-informed classrooms also serve as spaces where educators acknowledge systems of oppression and historical disinvestments in predominantly Black and brown neighborhoods that lead to the erosion of social and economic safety nets. It's of vital importance that educators grapple with race, confront their own biases, challenge stereotypes, and address inequality head-on. The commitment entails a vigilant, educated stance and the ability to offer comfort and guidance to children who struggle with the manifestations of these entrenched oppressive systems. Many teachers, particularly wealthy, privileged Black, Latine, or white teachers, must be made aware of what it means to teach traumatized kids.

In light of this, I propose a simple yet transformative solution: let's all commit to the journey of becoming lifelong learners. As the education landscape continues to evolve, it's our individual responsibility to continually educate ourselves, from books, from research, from those with lived experiences, from activists, and from our students and their families.

Being a lifelong learner means cultivating a state of beginner's mind. This Buddhist concept simply means that no matter your level of education or knowledge about a subject, you always place yourself in the mind of a beginner. The beginner is someone who's filled with curiosity and questions. They're completely open to new ideas and have no attachment to any specific way of doing things. This mindset allows us to be open to refining or even tossing out old methodology that doesn't support the changing and complex needs of children. By fostering a growth mindset, we can cultivate an atmosphere where all children feel seen, respected, and valued.

Engaging Students in Trauma-Informed Work

Like many other educators I know, I have a passion for learning. One thing that I'm always delightfully surprised by is the depth of knowledge that children bring to the classroom experience. While our knowledge about children can be extensive, and our intentions are to provide the best for them, it's critically important to prioritize including students in decision-making or curriculum planning since all that we do affects them. Together, we can drive meaningful changes within school communities where every child feels acknowledged, supported, and heard.

A foundation of trauma-informed practices lies in actively listening to students and sincerely responding to their needs and concerns. We must engage youth as equal partners meaningfully and authentically in the discovery, planning, implementation, and evaluation stages of youth-serving programs. By including students in positive and comprehensive conversations, we help in changing mindsets for both students and educators.

The US Department of Health and Human Services offers an excellent resource for giving students a chance to be a part of making decisions in their Listen Up! toolkit. I recommend giving it a read, but a brief outline of the process looks like this:

- *Planning a Youth Listening Session (YLS):* This involves setting goals and understanding the purpose of the session, deciding on the format (such as focus groups, interviews, writing workshops, or others), developing necessary materials, and recruiting and incentivizing youth participants.

- *Conducting a Youth Listening Session:* Once in the session, the teachers act as a moderator, guiding the students through the activities and conversations that are created in the planning process.

- *Acting on Youth Listening Sessions insights:* A formal debrief must follow each session, so the teachers can offer general reflections on what went well, what didn't, and what was learned. Then, action steps can be identified—and importantly—followed through on. Children spend almost all of their time under someone's thumb. Adults often demand that students follow arbitrary rules that sometimes don't make sense and seem made up. Involving students in the decision-making process gives them back some of their autonomy and shows them that their input really does matter; and that they can create change.

Practices that involve student input can be as varied as daily goal-setting, organizational methods, plans for regulating emotions, time for expressing joy through celebration and gratitude, and time and space for breaks. The more students feel that they have control over their day, the more they are going to be invested in how that day goes.

Engaging students at all levels of lesson planning and implementation helps kids to understand and know that they are equal partners in their own education. Beyond just what happens in the classroom, allowing students to be part of the short- and long-term strategic goals of the district and of the school can also help build the overall climate and culture of schools. Not all students want to become a part of the process, but you never know until you extend them an invitation.

School Safety

The work of educating children isn't rocket science, nor is it magic. For several years now, teacher professional development has included elements of Bloom's Taxonomy, which shows a continuous progression of how knowledge can be mastered and utilized successfully. This is a very educationally goal-oriented hierarchy of mental engagement, but it doesn't speak to barriers to that engagement. To understand those barriers, one must look to the ideology of Maslov, whose Hierarchy of Needs states that until basic physiological needs (food, water, housing, etc.) and the need for safety are met, nothing else can be accomplished. The theory comes down to the idea that basic needs must be met before true learning can occur and before there can be any form of Actualization, which is the highest level of the hierarchy. Only then can we expect students to engage with the depth of knowledge that Bloom's Taxonomy outlines.

Unfortunately, many students aren't getting their most basic physiological and safety needs met. They are hungry. They are homeless. They are often navigating unsafe spaces, both at home and in their neighborhoods. They feel endangered by violence at home, in the community, and sometimes in school. Where possible, I encourage teachers to give kids a meal or snack, let them take a nap, or offer them a simple hug (check your school district's policies on this); simple remedies like these can help students in the classroom, but there are also changes that can be made to the school at large.

The least that schools can do is be intentional about keeping children safe. School safety cannot be an afterthought; it must be given the highest priority, especially considering numerous and tragic school shootings. Importantly, making schools safer doesn't mean more police or more restrictive and punitive rules.

Take the issue of School Resource Officers. They began popping up in the 1950s as an attempt to foster relationships between police and students. Their presence in US schools has grown exponentially with the unfortunate rise of mass and school shootings. Their continued growth is evident in an online article written by James Patterson and published by the National Education Association (NEA). Under the heading, "Making Schools Safe and Just," Patterson states: "In 1975, only 1 percent of US schools reported having SROs, but that number rose to about 36 percent by 2004, and to 58 percent by 2018, including 72 percent of high schools. These increases are due in large part to more than $1 billion in federal funding to SROs."

Sadly, increasing the number of police in schools doesn't make children of color safer. This claim has been reinforced in a rather startling article, "Criminalizing Kids: When School call Police on Kids," written by Corey Mitchell et al. The article claims that "analysis of US Department of Education data from all fifty states plus the District of Columbia and Puerto Rico found that school policing disproportionately affects students with disabilities,

Black children, and in some states, Native American and Latino children." In economically disadvantaged communities and communities of color, interactions with police are historically more likely to be negative, traumatizing, or even deadly. Even just the presence of law enforcement in schools can be a source of trauma for some children. This isn't to say that every police officer in school buildings is a bad cop—that's far from the truth. I've witnessed meaningful and healthy relationship with an officer, specifically a Black police officer, who engaged with the students in his school, even while holding students to high behavioral standards.

Back home in Jamaica, we have a saying: "Mi an' police ah nuh fren," which means that the police are not our friends and are not welcome in our community. This is because of historical and perpetually oppressive police presence in lower-income neighborhoods. In some communities, common interaction with the police might even mark a person as a snitch, putting them at risk for retaliation, even death. Police are so mistrusted in some communities that mere polite socialization is taboo.

It's important to understand that the police are not inherently our enemies and that we do need law enforcement to maintain order and safety. However, the cultures and perceptions around policing need to change. We do this, firstly, by taking some of that power out of the hands of police and putting it into the hands of mental health service providers. Secondly, we do this by requiring culturally responsive and trauma-aware training for all police officers, especially the ones placed in our schools and in communities where mostly children of color reside. These initiatives can build trust within the school and broader community that they serve.

High-quality culturally, ethnically, and linguistically sensitive training helps law enforcement better understand the unique dynamics and challenges of the children they serve, especially those from diverse cultural backgrounds. These trainings promote empathy and sensitivity, reduce stress and trauma for kids, and make for a healthy and compassionate school. Finally, having a robust and responsive Multi-Tiered System of Supports (MTSS), the framework which helps struggling students behaviorally, socially, and emotionally, should take precedence over Resource Officers. This will help all children thrive in a trauma-informed school.

What School Districts Can Do to Help Educators

In an earnest pursuit to help and support teachers amid challenges, school districts play a pivotal role. It's paramount for district leaders and school administrators to embark on a journey of self-education, fostering a profound understanding of the intricate nuances of secondary trauma. Armed with this awareness, they can then align their efforts with the deliberate intention of nurturing their staff rather than overburdening them with impromptu demands, relentless cycles of testing preparations, and the often-dreaded teacher evaluations—which often fall short of authentically gauging pedagogical expertise.

To proactively support and mitigate so many of the stressors teachers experience, school districts can initiate a series of pragmatic, cost-effective steps that are both feasible and impactful. If not already undertaken, these steps can be seamlessly integrated into current practices to create an immediate positive influence on teacher and staff well-being. For example, making mental health services readily accessible within school settings for staff as well as students is a great benefit that schools can offer. Protecting mental health would, in my humble opinion, reduce educator absenteeism and make for more resilient teachers who can support the children in their classrooms more effectively.

Here are some tips for administrators to consider when meeting with teachers:

- *Be present when your teacher requests a meeting with you.* Practice active listening—not working on the computer, not multitasking. Active listening includes your body language, such as eye contact, which will let teachers know that they have your unwavering focus and attention.

- *Be empathetic and genuinely compassionate.* Let your teachers know that you appreciate them, and you are supporting them in every and any way you can.

- *Foster an environment where your staff feel empowered to prioritize their health and well-being* by taking the time they need for self-care. Advocate for mental health days to be regarded as vitally important as sick days, acknowledging that teachers' ability to effectively support students hinges upon their own well-being being nurtured and cared for.

- *Cultivate a profound sense of trust in your teachers and classroom staff,* including invaluable teacher assistants. Recognize teacher assistants as important and valued members of the teaching team.

- *Cultivate a robust and wholesome climate and culture within your school,* where every individual in the building is not only acknowledged but also cherished, esteemed, and treated with profound respect.

- *Ensure that every voice, irrespective of race, gender, religion, or sexual orientation, is not only heard but genuinely listened to,* fostering an inclusive environment that uplifts, empowers, and is a win-win for all.

- *Deliver ongoing professional training and staff development that's meticulously tailored* using staff input to meet the unique needs of your teaching and support staff.

- *Acknowledge that a one-size-fits-all approach may not yield optimal results,* as what proves effective in one region of the state or country may not necessarily translate to success in another school, state, or region.

- *Facilitate meaningful avenues for your staff to engage with the community and tap into its abundant resources.* Enrich their understanding by organizing insightful field trips that enable them to intimately interact with the very community where they invest substantial portions of their work week and where their students live. This immersive experience will not only forge stronger connections to families and the broader community but will also grant teacher and staff invaluable insights into the dynamics and needs of the children they teach.

- *Proactively introduce an array of resources and resource personnel to your school environment,* fostering a deep familiarity among your staff with the diverse services at their disposal. These services range from mental health services to emergency food provisions, free swimming opportunities, and beyond. Such offerings are pivotal for enriching the well-rounded support your school provides. By integrating these resources, you are empowering your staff to better serve their students' holistic needs.

- *Strive for a consistently balanced workload that upholds the principles of equity.* While achieving perfect equilibrium might be challenging, it remains imperative for school administrators to exert dedicated efforts in order to maintain a sense of fairness and balance in the distribution of tasks.

- *Wholeheartedly commemorate both significant milestones and minor victories within your school community.* Dedicate time to exuberantly applaud the efforts of your teachers and school staff, ensuring their achievements take center stage. Amplify their accomplishments through various channels, employing your "Bull Horn" to resound their successes. I can't tell you how eager I am to read my school's staff bulletin from my principal; it certainly energizes me and sets me on the path to more success. This practice not only fosters a robust sense of school spirit but also provides your staff with a powerful coping mechanism against the challenges of secondary trauma.

The Future is Now

As a former member of the House of Representatives, I would be remiss if I didn't devote some space to how change can come about on a broader level. The systemic oppression of children and their families living in poverty is perpetrated by a patriarchal apparatus that strategically and intentionally denies children and families basic necessities like clean air, food, healthcare, and housing needs. This needs to be dismantled, not reformed. The eradication of these oppressive systems is the only path toward ending the perpetual cycle of trauma that we see in classrooms all across our beautiful country.

To achieve this monumental task, it's essential that we select and elect folks at every tier of government: school committees, city council, state legislatures, and executive and judicial branches of government. We must elect leaders who have the profound ability to recognize the intrinsic capacity of every child and every individual, regardless of race, class, bloodline, religion, gender, or ethnic background.

While I understand better than most that the governmental process is slow and often infuriating, if you are someone with the power to vote, that power isn't one you should take for granted. Your vote does matter. You can make a difference for the children in your community. Do your research and vote in every election: vote for candidates who share your values. Change is possible.

I frequently found myself grappling with frustration as I tried to persuade my former colleagues in the legislature of the feasibility and wisdom of enacting legislation such as good commonsense gun safety laws, passing a $15 living wage, reducing out-of-school suspensions, or simply creating air quality standards. These initiatives—actual examples of legislation I worked on—consistently and vehemently encountered resistance from politicians who stubbornly favored corporate interest over the well-being of the people who elected them. The battle that I've had to engage in has been tough, but I've survived. Just because the fight is difficult doesn't mean we give up. In Chapter 7, I outline the work that went into getting the Trauma-Informed School Act passed as an example of what kind of perseverance is necessary.

Being trauma-informed is not a mere accumulation of hours or a certificate to showcase on a desk or in a portfolio. The essence of a trauma-informed educator transcends the confines of formal training. To be trauma-informed signifies an awakening, an understanding, and a profound empathy for complex dynamics that shape the lives of children grappling with poverty-induced trauma and toxic stress. To be trauma-informed entails delving into children's vicarious experiences, equipped with not only knowledge but also practical skills in order to help the children sitting in your classroom. For teachers, especially those in high-poverty zip codes, trauma-informed education urges practitioners to adopt a compassionate equity lens, fostering a proactive stance in addressing classroom challenges, fostering emotional regulation, and nurturing healing spaces for all students.

The solutions that I'm proposing are not herculean tasks. They are pragmatic fixes to address structural disparities and education inequality not just in our country but globally. If rich people can embark on extravagant joy rides to space, then they can help to end global child hunger and poverty, thus reducing trauma. In the next chapter, we'll look at taking the definitions I've provided here and putting them to work in real-life situations.

Helpful Hints from Teachers

- *Establish predictability and display norms that you and your students created.* This will help students understand classroom expectations, thereby setting them up for success.

- *Create safe spaces for children to help with emotional regulation.* I love that students at my school can have quiet lunches, especially those who suffer from anxiety.

- *Building trust and not over-promising is very important to all human beings,* including our children.

- *Practicing mindfulness, including deep breathing, helps students center and regulate.*

- *Practice empathy and kindness for everyone in your life,* including strangers. Empathy means you are accepting the whole person, not judging or pitying their situation.

- *Maintain a strong sense of humor.* Have fun with your kids and laugh. They need to see your joy, and it doesn't mean that you're a pushover.

CHAPTER 6

TRAUMA-INFORMED WORK IN ACTION

BEING TRAUMA-INFORMED is a win-win for everyone. Being trauma-informed helps us to anticipate the manifestations of trauma responses in school settings and provide compassionate responsive actions to attention-seeking or disruptive behaviors. This chapter takes a look at a few "case studies"—situations that I or teachers I've worked with have experienced.

As you'll see, there's a reason for every reaction that a child may have, even if it isn't plainly visible to the eyes. Through using trauma-informed techniques, there's a response to every situation that can defuse tension and, most importantly, let children know that we see them. Together, we can build strong, healthy, caring relationships with students and others in the school community.

Let's walk through these stories together.

Sylvia

Sylvia is a seasoned English teacher who has spent her entire career teaching in one of the toughest cities in an urban core community.

Whether it was by design or a fortuitous twist of fate, one year, her roster was filled with a rambunctious group of boys who liked to horse around with each other.

After reviewing her class rosters, Sylvia took note of the fact that most of the children came from households that made them eligible for either free or reduced lunches. Their neighborhoods were marked with gun violence and poverty, and there was a power plant emitting fumes right into the library where most of the boys went for after-school tutoring or enrichment activities. Further, more than a few of the children were being raised by single mothers. This isn't an anomaly; US Census Bureau (2022) data estimates that there are 10.9 million one-parent family groups with a child under the age of 18. The data also indicates that 80 percent of one-parent family groups were maintained by a mother.

Aware of the potential trauma that her students may have experienced, and the possible behavioral effects of that trauma, Sylvia was deliberate in her approach to every class. First, she commenced each period with a diverse genre of music, from rock and roll to Reggae, Merengue, classical, country, and Latin music, encouraging the kids to dance, yell, and move around.

Beyond exposing the kids to genres of music and artists they might not have previously known, this strategy yielded remarkable results. Students in her classroom were better able to concentrate after they had settled into class, and although she had a curriculum that was rigorous, the level of stress in her classroom dropped dramatically. Her results are backed up by a study published in *Frontiers in Psychology*, which asserted that "music can also play a role in helping individuals and communities to cope with trauma, whether it be through the intervention of music therapists, community music making programs or individual music listening."

Sylvia's approach was two-fold: she aimed to provide her students with the benefit of a challenging curriculum while remaining acutely aware of the traumatic experiences they lived with every day. Her use of music as a trauma-informed practice was an intentional attempt to offer support and solace to her students. At the same time, she enabled them to more fully access the rich curriculum in a safe and loving classroom culture.

Jay

It was a regular midweek day at the Bridge School where I worked, but we had some leftover pizza from parent-teacher conferences the previous night. I put out the pizza so the kids could enjoy it, but as soon as Jay saw the pizza, he exclaimed, "This is white people food. Where's the chitlins at? Where's the fry chicken?"

Before I had time to think or even ask him what he was talking about, he kicked over several chairs and tossed all of the leftovers right in the garbage. He was erratic and out of control. To my surprise, there was a round of applause from his classmates.

I found myself standing in the classroom, speechless. What was I supposed to do to quell this potential uprising over what was deemed "white people food"?

With a composed, steady, and calm voice, I looked him in the eyes and asked, "Why did you do that, Jay?"

His response was straightforward, delivered with a mischievous grin on his beautiful, round face. "Because I'm bad."

Jokingly, I told him, "Well, I'm from Kingston, Jamaica, and I'm 'badder' than you are, an' I run things in this school."

He cracked up, laughing, then gave me a big hug. That settled that. A bit of humor certainly brought the temperature down and eased the tension.

This could have easily gotten out of hand or landed Jay in hot water, but especially with all the children watching, I knew I needed to deescalate.

I share this interaction to underscore the need to be able to respond in ways students do not expect. When students act out, they expect negative attention, and to deescalate, a teacher must go in the opposite direction.

I chose to laugh with the kids, to just be funny and let them know that I was human. I may not be the funniest teacher to walk the face of the Earth, but God knows, and my students do too, that I love to be jovial. My joke not only sought to lighten the mood but also to remind Jay that I wasn't just a representative of a cold institution he could rail against: I was a human with my own experiences. So, that simple, calm response released tension in the classroom and lightened the space so we could get back to the important work of teaching and learning.

I also learned something from Jay that day: his culture mattered greatly to him, and he wanted to see it represented in his classroom. Moving forward, I made sure that when I had an event at the school, I was intentional to have food that was representative of all my students' cultures. I started doing more to celebrate the rainbow of cultures and ethnicities in my classroom. This is why we did a project to decorate the classroom with flags from countries all over the world, and I also encouraged students to bring in books and other literature that they read at home. I was eager to be culturally responsive, creating a space where each child's culture was represented and where they felt a sense of belonging.

Over the years, I've stayed in touch with Jay and looked out for him while making sure that he was supported. The last time he called, he was looking for a job, and I connected him to someone who was able to help him. I'm happy to report that he's working and raising a beautiful little boy of his own.

Kerry

Kerry was a senior in high school. She was one of a handful of Caucasian students in Hampton High. She was popular, with a tight-knit group of friends who'd stuck together since freshman year. Midway into her senior year, her physics teacher, Mr. Keene, noticed a significant change in her demeanor. Kerry had become increasingly withdrawn, often hiding beneath her hoodie. She also stopped attending after-school tutoring and the tennis club that she had previously enjoyed.

Realizing the change, Mr. Keene checked in to let Kerry know he was genuinely concerned about her well-being. Between tears, Kerry told her teacher that her mom suffered from schizophrenia, and it had gotten really bad. She was worried that her mom might harm herself or even harm her. In response, Mr. Keene offered his heartfelt comfort and support. He immediately referred her to the school's social work department, which would be better able to provide additional support and help, including other resources.

Mr. Keene's response was timely and incredibly appropriate. It was evident from Kerry's willingness to open up and share her deeply personal concerns that she had a healthy and trusting relationship with her teacher. She confided to him about the challenges and concerns that she had regarding her mother's health and safety. She also shared how it was impacting her own mental health.

Supporting kids in crisis truly necessitates a team effort, and Mr. Keene exemplified this. He knew immediately that Kerry needed someone to confide in, but she also needed so much more. Realizing that he didn't possess the necessary skills to help his student, he connected her to other team members at the school, and Kerry was able to quickly get the help, guidance, and support that she needed. With assistance, her mom began to improve, and Kerry felt safe again and was able to reclaim her joy in school activities.

Being trauma-informed entails not only having the knowledge of trauma and its impact on students but also being readily able to access necessary resources in a timely fashion. If the school you work at doesn't have these resources, how can you advocate for them? Are there similar resources in the broader community that could be helpful? These are some questions to consider before a student is in immediate need of help.

Chad

Chad lived with his mom and dad. Family services were heavily involved with the family. There were allegations of abuse, including rape, and Chad had witnessed his mother being beaten by his father. From the time that he was eleven, Chad continually ran away from home. At school, he was known for his outbursts and uncontrollable temper. He never learned how to self-regulate. By the time he was in twelfth grade, he had only earned ten credits and was at risk of dropping out of high school. He had also become homeless, sleeping in cars and at bus stops on nights when he couldn't find a couch.

Luckily, Mr. Cox, a teacher's assistant, became the only stable person in Chad's life. Mr. Cox would help Chad out by getting his clothes washed and providing him with other essentials. He advocated for him every step of the way. When his teachers became frustrated with Chad, Mr. Cox would step in, taking him for walks and helping him regulate his emotions. Along with some of the teachers, Mr. Cox created a behavior plan, including modifications like going to the school store for snacks when needed, using his phone at school when he had completed modified assignments, and simply taking brain breaks.

Though things improved for Chad at school, he unfortunately didn't graduate and was even incarcerated as a young adult. But Mr. Cox didn't give up on him. He kept in touch with Chad and even reached out to the superintendent, who then helped Chad negotiate the prison system. While incarcerated, Chad earned his GED and began receiving mental health services. Of course, it wasn't the outcome that Mr. Cox had originally hoped for, but he strongly believes that Chad will be able to successfully integrate back into society once he completes his period of incarceration.

Dan

When Dan was a brand-new teacher, he had been recruited to fill the teacher shortage in one of the urban core cities of the northeast. He lived in one of the wealthiest neighborhoods in Rhode Island, and prior to teaching full-time in Providence, he hadn't even visited the city. His first interaction with poverty and kids who had experienced ACEs was when he landed a teaching job. When he started, he was so afraid of the kids, which is something that he says brings him a lot of shame now. Some of the fear came from his lack of adequate training in teaching kids who were exposed to trauma.

At first, he thought he had to be tough with the kids and let them know that he was in charge. He'd just graduated from college and was eager to teach the kids all the scientific knowledge that he'd learned. The more he piled on, the less engaged and more disruptive they became. Students would yell, throw things, and be uncooperative, while others were simply withdrawn. Dan lost control of his ninth-grade class and was calling the office continually, which only seemed to make them respect him even less. He knew that they weren't learning. He knew that the kids needed help, but he simply wasn't sure what kind.

Frustrated, he turned to the school psychologist, Mr. Henry, who gave him as much help as he could, including frequent check-ins and pulling disruptive kids out of the class. It was like using your finger to block a hole in a dam; it helped the immediate issue, but the disruptions and disrespect continued.

Dan said he felt like a loser, but he didn't want to quit. He didn't want to give up on the kids. He decided to read everything that he could about kids growing up in poverty. It was through reading that he began to realize how traumatic the lives of some of the children in his class were. He found a wealth of strategies to help him not just cope with the children but to fall in love with them. It was during his years of continued learning that he realized that he didn't have to be tough; he needed to build relationships with the students. By becoming more aware of what was going on in their day-to-day lives, he could tailor his instruction to their needs. Dan ended up spending twenty-nine years working as a teacher in Providence. Though he initially retired, he's now in his second stint as a long-term substitute teacher in the city and is loving it.

Aaron

Only fifteen, Aaron was a tall, slim boy with a smile that would light up the room—except he rarely smiled. He seemed angry all the time. He came from a pretty violent home where he'd witnessed his father abusing his mom and experienced verbal abuse from his father, who was later incarcerated. They lived in a two-bedroom house in a densely populated area of the city that was prone to violence, including burglaries and homicides. Although his mom worked odd jobs, they were barely able to make ends meet. For these reasons, Aaron ended up in state care regularly.

His teacher, Sydney, knew that his anger, frustration, detachment, and resentment of authority were a symptom of everything he'd been through. She tried to connect with him, but nothing was working. He even called her an "ugly white bi*ch" during one of her classes. Then, something clicked. She discovered that he loved to read. She got to know the books he liked and made sure to incorporate them into her classes. She noticed how his eyes lit up every time they studied a novel, and she provided lots of opportunities to talk about literature.

Sydney was also acutely aware of the disproportionate number of out-of-school suspensions that students in state and foster care received. She knew things were hard for Aaron at home, and whenever possible, she didn't report him to administration when he ran afoul of the school contract. Instead, she worked quietly with the social work team to support him. It was then that she began to notice small but encouraging improvements in his behavior.

Fred

I've known Gina for over ten years, and she's a compassionate, veteran social worker of thirteen years. In addition to providing social work counseling, Gina and her colleagues set up a hygiene counter where kids are at liberty to take what they need. She also works with Fred, who's a licensed therapy dog. They work together at the largest school district in her home state of Rhode Island, which has a student population of close to 13,000 students. I was thrilled that she agreed to a sit-down interview with me.

Anyone with a pet knows how wonderful they can be, and working with a dog in school is very rewarding for Gina. Fred is great at helping kids regulate emotions; sometimes, it's as easy as having kids touch and gently pet the dog. Fred provides comfort for students who may be hungry, had a fight with family members prior to school beginning, or who may have heard gunshots in their neighborhood the night before. He even helps parents. At one meeting, Gina recalls that as a parent was yelling, Fred became agitated, so the parent immediately calmed down, feeling sorry for him.

After coming back to school after COVID, Gina noted that teachers were stressed and needed comfort, and Fred was able to offer that. Gina noted that if teachers are experiencing a lot of stress, whether inside or outside of school, they bring those emotions to school. This stress impacts their ability to be effective. Gina strongly believes that with the escalating incidences of mental health crises, every school should have a Fred—his presence provides peace and opens the door for teaching, learning, and healing.

###

I hope that these "case studies" show how utilizing trauma-informed practices in the classroom provides more opportunities for every school to improve teaching, learning, and healing. With the right support, kids can actually thrive, and that's what this work is all about.

A word of caution: trauma-informed practices are not one-size-fits-all. What worked with one student might not work with another. The technique one teacher uses might not work for you. The basis for success lies in relationship building. Know your students and actively plan for their success. Remember to keep an open mind and get curious about each student as an individual. What lights them up? What sets them off? This way, you can tailor your response in the classroom and make real connections with them.

The next rung on the ladder is implementing trauma-informed practices school-wide. It isn't enough for just one person to have a connection to a student; there must be a network of support and an active school culture where all children feel safe, supported, cared for, and loved. So, in the next chapter, we'll explore the Trauma-Informed School Act.

Helpful Hints from Teachers

- *Listen to quiet music throughout your class periods.*

- *Always have a plan.* You are there to help create structure and order that may be missing from your students' lives.

- *Be willing to share power in your classroom* so that everyone is invested in how the day goes. This can be easily done through inclusive language, such as "our classroom" instead of "my classroom."

- *Go over the school safety plans* on your own and know them backward and forward.

- *Ask for help; only strong people do.* Collaboration is key when protecting yourself and your students from trauma. The case studies in this chapter show that we all have different skills and needs. Find someone who knows what you don't to help you better serve students.

CHAPTER 7

PASSING THE TRAUMA-INFORMED SCHOOL ACT

"MAR, YOU USE the word *fight* a lot. Why are you always fighting?"

I pondered the question that my youngest sister, Lisa, asked me. She's more practical and filtered than I am. Her words sank deep into my heart, plunging me into deep reflection. She's right— I'm always fighting for the common good. I throw all of myself into this work advancing justice, but justice and fighting come at a price. It doesn't matter how tough you think you are; fighting takes a physical and emotional toll on your body. Truth be told, it's hard, but children are worth fighting for. I won't stop until I take my last breath. However, I must remember to take care of myself. I'm trying.

Reflecting on my life, growing up in poverty, experiencing gun violence, and enduring periods of hunger has taught me the lesson of survival. My experiences have uniquely shaped the person I am today; they have shaped my ideology and caused me to see the world using an equity and trauma-informed lens. These perspectives afford me a distinctive vantage point, one that aligns me closely with students who are grappling with systemic and structural issues of poverty.

Schools, like all other institutions in the United States and around the world, aren't immune to systemic failures. It's a stark reality, but children living in poverty, particularly Black, brown, and Indigenous, and children in foster care, frequently find themselves feeling disconnected from schools that don't always provide safety or a sense of belonging. During my time as an elected official, I focused on helping to change systems, laws, and policies that created formidable barriers to kids experiencing the joy of learning and achieving success. My plan while in the assembly was to work with others who shared my values. Together, we worked night and day to dismantle oppressive systems and promote the potential well-being and growth of our students.

Entering the Political Arena

I had no aspirations for political office. I was living my life caring for my family when a young twenty-one-year-old was shot and killed. When I launched my improbable 2016 campaign for State Representative in House District 5, my tagline was "Marcia ... Fighting For All of Us." The succinct phrase encapsulated my unwavering commitment to my constituents who desperately needed critical investments and resources to pull themselves out of poverty. I was in it for the people, for the working class, and for the poor. I wanted to dismantle the status quo that was working for the well-connected few.

At my core, I'm a teacher, not a politician, and that realization guided my path. I had fought for my seat; I understood the assignment. I don't think it was a coincidence that I was assigned seat number 12. I think of Jesus Christ and his twelve disciples, their purpose being to attend to the needs of poor and marginalized communities and to comfort those who are brokenhearted. I felt that this was a part of my spiritual journey in life, and I was determined to make the best of it.

I yearned for the day when politics serve the people and politicians serve the constituents who elected them instead of fat cats and corporations. I came face to face with this reality during my very first week in the House of Representatives. It quickly became apparent that I lacked the appetite for the intricate maneuvering, the jostling, that was necessary in the arena. I recognized quite early that the predominantly white space had the potential to drain the life out of me and it was important for me to guard my overall health and well-being.

My first term in office proved to be a very challenging one. I decided not to vote for the then-Speaker of the House, instead siding with a group of Progressive Democrats. It was not a political move but rather a move based on values that essentially set the tone for the rest of my inaugural year. After that initial vote, no matter how much I tried, I couldn't get one piece of legislation to the House Floor for an up or down vote. I was completely blocked out. The prevailing norm was to toe the party line or risk facing consequences, often in the form of having one's legislative agenda sidelined. In spite of this, I introduced bill after bill. My mission was clear: to advocate for students and their families who had been historically marginalized. Here's a brief look at a few of the bills I championed.

The Fight for $15

A critically important piece of legislation I introduced was HB-7636, which would raise the minimum wage to $15 per hour. Although this specific bill wasn't considered for passage at the time, over the next several years, the minimum wage has been raised incrementally. By 2025, the minimum wage will be raised to $15 an hour.

The significance of this legislation in the context of trauma and trauma-informed schooling cannot be overstated—it's interconnected in every way. Children whose parents are unable to make a living wage are also unable to provide the basic necessities, resulting in children experiencing hunger, a lack of clean clothing, periods of homelessness, and potential exploitation and assaults. Lower-income children also experience higher rates of bullying or ostracization in the school community. The ripple effect of increasing the minimum wage extends far beyond economics. Increasing the minimum wage would help reduce chronic absenteeism, close the knowledge and skills gap, promote family and child mental health and well-being, as well as give families upward social mobility.

Ending Lunch Shaming

I strongly believe that food is a basic human right and every child who shows up in the school's cafeteria is entitled to a free, hot, nutritious lunch, no questions asked. The reality is that this isn't always the case and kids across the country are shamed and denied a free meal because of their family's inability to pay lunch debt. As a teacher, I know just how important it is to feed kids. Without food in their stomachs, kids are unable to concentrate in class and unable to learn.

I was brand new in the assembly when I received a call from a parent living in one of the most affluent areas of Rhode Island. Her child was denied lunch and had received an alternate meal. The call angered me. Instantaneously, I turned that anger into activism by introducing a bill in the spring of 2017 to end lunch shaming in all of Rhode Island's public schools. Seven years later, the legislature still refuses to pass this morally imperative bill. Meanwhile, seven states, including our closest neighbors, have passed similar bills. It irks me to know that Rhode Island could have been a national leader in how we feed and take care of all of our children. Rather, we trail behind, still wondering, "How are we going to pay for it?" Although I have introduced the bill every year during my time in office, I remain committed to this fight for free, accessible, and healthy foods. It's my hope that one day those in positions of power and influence will recognize the vital connections between food access and students' academic, behavioral, and social outcomes.

Extreme Risk Protection Order

In response to the critical need to provide enhanced support for individuals grappling with mental health issues, I introduced a comprehensive and balanced approach to addressing the crisis that has taken too many innocent lives. HB-7763: Extreme Risk Protection Order (ERPOs), often known as the "Red Flag bill," would provide district courts with the authority to "temporarily seize firearms from anyone believed to be in immediate danger to themselves or others." Although my bill didn't make it to the House Floor, a similar bill did. I'm happy to report that Rhode Island now has implemented the law, and as of 2023, twenty-one states plus Washington D.C. have Red Flag laws on the books.

You Can't Talk About Guns, Marcia

I was extremely fervent about a progressive resolution that would examine the trauma experienced by kids who had one or both parents incarcerated or who were exposed to the pervasive and devastating effects of gun violence. This resolution spoke to my deep commitment to addressing some of the root causes of trauma and adversity that many students experience. Having a parent in prison can have an impact on a child's mental health, social behavior, and educational prospects. I've seen the harsh reality of this type of separation. Losing a parent to the prison complex often means that kids are transferred to state care or placed in group homes. I've also seen kids lash out and become rebellious in response to the incarceration of a parent. In all the scenarios, there's definitely an impact on kids' mental health and, by extension, on their education. Children of incarcerated parents may also be more likely to face other adverse childhood experiences, including witnessing violence in their communities or directly in their households.

After meeting with the Speaker, I was told that any bill that had verbiage mentioning guns, like one related to gun violence and incarceration, would be too divisive and my colleagues would never support such a bill. He suggested that I take out the word "gun" and just create a bill that was more generally about researching the effects of trauma. Anxious to have the legislation passed that would examine the impact of trauma on kids, I revised the bill and introduced HB-7613: A House Resolution to Create a Special Legislative Commission to Study the Impact of the Trauma Inflicted on Children who are Exposed to Violence. By passing this resolution, we would be setting our students up for lifelong success and creating pathways where they could grow and thrive while also recovering from horrible stress and uncertainties.

Over the course of the next five years, the bill met its demise—a fate common to many promising pieces of legislation that prioritized children and their families. This unfortunate outcome was the result of the prevailing political landscape. While the Speaker had supported many of my efforts, including funding for my district's community summer programs for youth as well as grant money to replace the old and dilapidated furniture at my local library, I don't believe that he wanted to challenge or agitate the gun lobby which supported him.

Keep in mind that this was a time when the issue of trauma and children's mental health was not talked about as much in the public sphere. Not acting on this legislation underscored the challenging environment in which legislators and advocates like myself were striving to pass legislation that would support not only our students facing mental health challenges but also their teachers and support staff in schools.

The Trauma-Informed Schools Act

I keep my equity lens on all the time. With that focus, every single bill that I introduced during my six years in the assembly took into consideration the intersectionality of trauma on all of our lives, but more importantly, on the lives of children—particularly the most vulnerable. So, it will come as no surprise that I was most zealously committed to HB-6667: The Trauma-Informed Schools Act.

By putting this Act forward, my hope was that the knowledge gleaned from this law would equip teachers, administrators, and related service providers with the knowledge and skills necessary to better serve kids who are exposed to traumatic experiences. In addition, my ultimate goal was that the resolution would lay the foundation for a study commission tasked with developing a comprehensive, statewide trauma-informed curriculum. Such a curriculum would be the first of its kind in Rhode Island and a transformative step toward fostering school environments of understanding, empathy, healing, and empowerment for teachers and all of their students.

As hard as I tried, I just couldn't break through. I spent time trying to convince the Speaker of the House that we needed to pass my bill. He refused to budge, remaining non-committal.

I was devastated. I had no ulterior motives; I simply wanted to help kids succeed.

I could feel the walls closing in around me, the water rising above my head. I realized that if I was going to get anything done, I would have to play the political game, as much as I didn't want to. I called up Senator Sam Bell, who had been the Senate sponsor of the bill from the very beginning. Typically, each bill has a sponsor for both the House and Senate chambers. Sam was a supporter of mine as well as an agitator in the fairly conservative Senate chamber and its leadership. But, if anyone could help, it was Sam.

"Hey, Sam," I said, "I need your help. I really need to have the trauma bill passed, and the Senate President will not pass it out of committee with you as the Prime Sponsor. I'm going to ask Senator Cano to be the Prime Sponsor. I know how hard you've worked on this, but we need to get this thing done for the kids."

Without hesitation, Sam wholeheartedly agreed. There are moments in life when one needs to demonstrate one's ability to bend and not break; leadership must take precedent. I'm forever grateful for Sam Bell's unwavering support and devotion in this cause and so many others. After our short conversation, I immediately called Senator Cano and told her of the strategy.

Senator Cano is a dedicated Latina and respected champion of many children's issues. She was more than happy to support the bill. With her on board, we continued the righteous fight. I escalated conversations with students and their families, delved into more research, and pursued and received training and certification in trauma-informed practices. To gain momentum, I formed partnerships with teachers, students, legislators, practitioners, and advocates, all united in the mission to ensure Rhode Island's education system became trauma-informed. From these connections, a brilliant group of about thirty participants all met together for weekly Zoom meetings to discuss strategies to move the bill out of committees and to the House and Senate Floors for a vote.

Our vision went well beyond the classroom. We aimed to provide trauma-informed training and support for all K-12 class-rooms as well as staff working in the child penal system, bus drivers, crossing guards, cafeteria workers, and school maintenance workers. The impact of trauma extends well beyond the confines of the classroom, and the only way to truly have a trauma-informed school system is if everyone's on the same page.

I worked hard, using social media, making phone calls, having conversations with my peers and advocates in and out of the legislature, and working strategically with the leadership team in the House of Representatives to have the bill passed. All of this was on top of my duties as a teacher! Senator Cano was simultaneously working strategically with her peers, advocates, and Senate leadership to get the bill moved across the finish line.

With steadfast determination and an outpouring of support, we rallied all available hands and hearts to advance our righteous cause. Our team of teachers, students, parents, mental health workers, and other concerned citizens contacted legislators, held a press conference, composed heartfelt letters, and talked to other constituents; we were all focused on spreading the word that there was an urgent need for trauma-informed legislation.

One evening in early 2022, I was walking to the second floor of the State House, my heart heavy from the weight of my mission, when the new Speaker of the House, K. Joseph Shekarchi, asked me, "Marcia, how important is the trauma bill to you?" Without a minute to even think and my eyes welling up with tears, I emphatically responded, "Very important. It's the most important bill of my entire tenure, Speaker."

"Then you got it," he replied. This meant the bill would have the Speaker's full support and would be headed to the House Floor for a vote. Overwhelmed with emotions, I returned to my desk and wept with disbelief and joy. Would this endeavor that I'd poured my heart and soul into since April 2017 finally come to fruition? I was picturing all my students' faces already lit up at the possibilities that it would offer them.

While I believe the Speaker's intentions were entirely policy-driven—plus, he also knew how much this piece of legislation meant to me and how hard I'd worked over the years—I also believe that he hadn't forgotten that his ascension to the speakership came as a result of me defeating the former speaker. Speaker Shekarchi and I continue to have a good relationship, marked by mutual respect, which I hope continues to center the needs of all children and their families.

I dressed up in my power color red for the big moment my bill would hit the floor. Without fanfare, House Bill 6667 Sub A was approved on May 18, 2022, with fifty-nine of sixty-four representatives present voting for the bill. Five Republican representatives voted "No." Then, Senate Bill 2556 Sub B was approved on June 21, 2022, with thirty-five Senators voting "Yes" and a lone Republican present voting "No."

It was clear to me that while I'd been introducing this bill for several years, and I personally knew that childhood trauma wasn't a new issue, the huge increase in challenges that students were facing because of the pandemic made this issue forefront for other legislators as well. The month before, the Rhode Island Chapter of the American Academy of Pediatrics, along with several other health organizations, declared a mental health state of emergency for Rhode Island's children, saying the "worsening crisis in child and adolescent mental health is inextricably tied to the stress brought on by COVID-19 and the ongoing struggle for racial justice, and represents an acceleration of trends observed prior to 2020."

Having passed both legislative chambers, the bill was signed into law by Governor Daniel McKee on June 30, 2022. A major part of the law was the empaneling of a Trauma-Informed Schools Commission. I thought my work was done and that the law was now a living, moving thing—but not so fast. It would take the next several months for the appointment of the twelve-member commission who would be in charge of helping the Department of Elementary and Secondary Education to implement the critical aspects of the new law. Again, I had to make calls to supporters of the new law, engage and advocate with allies on social media, and do all of the heavy lifting to get the commission off the ground. On February 22, 2023, the Rhode Island Department of Education (RIDE) empaneled the Trauma-Informed Schools Commission with twelve local, community, education, and mental health professionals. The Trauma-Informed Schools Act requires the establishment of a commission to assist the agency with the implementation of the statute. The commission was required to meet quarterly during fiscal years 2023–2024, and a final report is due by June 30, 2024.

I'm deeply appreciative that there's a Trauma-Informed Schools law in Rhode Island. However, I'm acutely aware that this is just the beginning—changes have not been implemented yet. With full implementation, students will have educators who are trained and supported to recognize signs of trauma and to create classroom environments lovingly and carefully. Once fully implemented, the law will also support teachers in their use of classroom management strategies rooted in trauma-informed practices to avoid re-traumatization of students.

Children are hurting; they are still in crisis and need urgent care. Per the Rhode Island Department of Education, Rhode Island is the number one state receiving Substance Abuse and Mental Health Services Administration (SAMHSA) funds. If that's so, then the funds must be utilized to adequately resource schools with more social workers, more guidance counselors, more culturally responsive training, and more mental health providers. I don't see where this is happening. I want to be convinced otherwise. Schools across this state, this country, and globally aren't adequately resourced to address the mental health needs of the children. Schools are understaffed and the staff they have need far more support. Right now, we're living in the moment where the rubber hits the road. The work is just starting—how will you support it?

Trauma Messes with Your Joy

I cannot leave this chapter without sharing my own struggles during this time. I got up on Thursday, August 18, the very day that Governor McKee was to sign the bill into law, and all I felt was a profound sense of sudden letdown. All the people who knew of the importance of the bill would be there at the signing. Yet, I didn't want to go.

I'd worked my butt off for over five years, and now that the bill was to be signed into law, I contemplated skipping the ceremonial signing. I was emotionally spent, and I knew it. I wanted to do what I'd done many times over, what I've watched students do: hide under my hoodie. Just hide.

Acknowledging joy in that moment, never mind embracing it, was difficult for me. I knew joy and happiness, but it felt like a distant memory. The exhaustion resulting from five-plus years of relentless frustration had taken a toll on me and wore me down mentally and emotionally. In my head, I knew that this feeling was the result of the trauma I'd been through. But my body didn't care. I just wanted to rest and be alone.

Not wanting to disappoint those around me, I pushed my way through, just like many traumatized children do. If I could just get there, I told myself, I knew I would be fine. I had a knack for showing up despite inner turmoil—a skill those of us who have experienced trauma know how to navigate. This time would be no different.

A million thoughts rushed through my mind as I drove down I-95. I felt far away, fully immersed in a sadness that went deep inside. I wanted to just disappear, but there was nowhere to go. As I entered the parking lot, people recognized and congratulated me. My lovely friend, Kate, was overjoyed and began videotaping me, singing, "Here comes my hero!" I hurried quickly to find the bathroom, hoping in a strange way that I could escape. I said a silent prayer: "Lord, I just want to thank you for today—this bill is going to save so many lives, including possibly my own."

I composed myself and walked back out to the area where family, friends, supporters, and elected officials, including Governor McKee, had congregated for the signing. After the speeches, the bill signing, the passing out of ceremonial pens, and the pictures, I still couldn't feel a thing. Nothing. Joy eluded me. I was numb. I got in the car and headed home, only to find that I'd lost my ceremonial signing pen (though it turned up later in my sister's pocketbook). It all felt like a letdown.

So why am I sharing this? I'm sharing this because trauma steals our joy, even when we achieve our goals. It makes us numb, detached from the moment, and even wanting to escape from events or beautiful memories. I'd expended so much emotional energy trying to pass this bill that my mind was still burdened by its pain. I didn't readily know how to detach myself so I could experience the joy of the fight being over.

Yes, fighting to pass the Trauma-Informed Schools Act was an uphill struggle, but I didn't do it alone. I'm glad we persevered and clawed and fought our way to this piece of justice. Now, it's up to the state to make it work for kids as well as teachers and other school personnel. I'm hopeful that with this law and the outcomes of the study commission, state and federal funding can be secured for more mental health services along with training for teachers, administrators, and paraprofessionals in trauma-informed teaching.

Helpful Hints from Teachers

- *Be consistent in your beliefs and routines,* but also be ready and willing to find flexibility as needed. Sometimes, we have to prioritize our goals and let go of what at first appears to be the only path.

- *Leave your work at school.* Set boundaries around work, activism, and home life, and treat them like they are precious.

- *Make time for mindfulness,* whether that means meditation, breathwork, a calming bath at the end of the week, drinking your first cup of coffee without multitasking, or anything else that works for you. Mindfulness can be anything that helps you focus on the present moment.

- *Know that you're a model* and that you have eyes watching every move you make. This might be in your own home, in the classroom, or if you choose to pursue political office.

- *Do your best each day* and remember that things might look different from day to day. Each morning represents a new start and a new perspective.

PART THREE

EMPOWERING CHANGE

CHAPTER 8

BEGIN WITH YOURSELF

CAROL, ONE OF the teachers at my school, sat at her desk and mumbled a few words to herself. "Carol, you're talking to yourself. Are you okay?" I asked probingly and with deep concern for her well-being. She hadn't been her usual lively self lately and was dealing with a series of personal setbacks. I wanted to make sure that I was being as supportive as I possibly could and was even checking in on those days when she wasn't in school.

"No, I'm pretty good," she responded. "I'm just thinking about my kids and all that they have been through. I'm just wondering if I'm enough, if I'm doing enough. Or if being more knowledgeable about adverse childhood experiences would help me become a better teacher." Her voice was filled with concern. "It's disheartening, but I've been teaching for over twenty-five years, and not a single course I took in college incorporated ACEs in its teacher education program. Heck, how am I supposed to be an effective teacher when I have no clue about what my kids experience? I just feel like I'm failing these children. Marcia, I feel like such a failure, a loser."

I could tell that Carol was not only upset but also that her frustration level had hit the roof—she felt that she'd failed. I moved closer to her desk and *kotched* on the edge of one of the desks, making sure I didn't fall. In my Jamaican culture, when anyone *kotches* (to sit on the edge of something), you know they are either ready to hear *labrish* (gossip), or they are ready to help. I was ready to help.

I reassured her, "Carol, you're an awesome teacher. I know you care about the kids—don't beat upon yourself. I know you want to learn more about the ACEs; I also know you want to learn more about what your students are going through. It takes time; it's a process. It takes conversations; it takes building empathy and self-compassion. So why don't we study and learn together?"

She looked at me, and in her eyes, I could tell she wanted to learn more, and I was there to help her.

Teaching is indeed a team sport and students benefit when they know their teachers care about each other, collaborate, share research and best practices, and remain in a supportive mode. After the conversation with Carol, I was careful not to let her feel like I was judging her in any way. Instead, I approached the situation with empathy and support.

I brought in a couple of books from my home library (see the Resources section for a list to get started!). I gave the books to her and chatted lightheartedly about life. I was cognizant of the fact that I didn't want to overwhelm her or make her feel inadequate. I didn't want her to think that I was positioning myself as an expert, but more so as a colleague who simply wanted to be supportive. I reassured Carol that, as a compassionate and kind teacher, she already possessed a wealth of knowledge about the challenges that her students faced and, like her, they would be okay too.

Perhaps you can relate to Carol. You're a teacher who cares about your students and sees them needing help, but you aren't quite sure what exactly it is that they need or what you can offer.

Where do you start?

You have to begin with yourself. And by that, I mean you need to have an understanding of where you're coming into this work and what you still need to learn. You need to know your *Why*. Even after decades in this work, I still find myself asking, "Why are you here, Mar?" Sometimes, as educators and paraprofessionals, we get so bogged down with the day-to-day work of fulfilling yet another unnecessary demand that gets piled onto our already overwhelming to-do list that we lose sight of what brought us to our careers. Sometimes, we're simply putting out fires and not taking the time to work on our craft in a way that improves our pedagogy or our understanding of teaching children.

Every teacher, paraprofessional, or administrator knows what a "Do Now" is. For those reading this book who aren't educators and may not be familiar with the terminology, a Do Now is the first activity teachers use to set the tone for success in their classroom.

In this chapter, I'll present a few activities that you, reader, can Do Now as you begin your exploration of trauma-informed self-care. I'll also offer some questions that you can return to on your journey toward becoming a trauma-informed educator. I'm sure that you will be able to add more to this list, but let's begin.

Be Your Own Cheerleader

Teaching kids is hard work, but it's also heart work. Be your own cheerleader! Sing, dance, and practice self-compassion while you hold yourself accountable for your personal and professional long- and short-term goals. Remind yourself how beautiful and awesome you are. At the end of the day, you may even want to buy yourself some flowers!

Get Yourself an Accountability Partner

Even with the best intentions of practicing self-care, it can be a daunting and herculean task if we try to do it alone. Having a trusted partner, colleague, or friend is a good way to hold us accountable and help us achieve our self-care goals. How many times have we paid for gym membership or promised ourselves that we're going to start eating healthier, and without even thinking, we fall off the wagon? How many times have we told ourselves that we're going leave work early or not take work home on weekends because we want to make time and space for ourselves or our families, yet we end up lugging home a book bag filled with essays to correct or sub-plans to write? Or, as a social worker once told me, "Even when we don't physically carry work home, we have all the work rent space in our heads," which keeps us up all night, unable to enjoy peace of mind or quiet time. Setting clear work hours for work and personal time is not a luxury; it's a necessity.

The truth is that these things are easier said than done. As educators, we have a mile-high list of things to do: problem-solving, trouble-shooting for students or colleagues, attending another unhelpful meeting on Zoom when we could be spending time cultivating and fostering friendships, collaborating with colleagues, speaking to a mental health counselor in our school that's available to staff, or writing gratitude notes to colleagues. Divorcing ourselves from our work is virtually impossible, but we must try. We must make time for going to the gym, going for walks, and doing activities that help to de-clutter our minds in order to experience peace and tranquility. Having someone to hold us accountable for what our personal self-preservation goals are is the most unselfish act that we can do for ourselves. Having someone we can trust helping us to create balance in our lives, encouraging us, and helping us affirm our own self-worth will ultimately help the students.

Choose Your Battles Carefully

As educators, we must commit to choosing our battles carefully and not "which hill you'll die on." Decide intentionally which tasks you'll take on in order of priority. For instance, I have a hard time delegating. I find it easier if I do the task by myself. I'm still learning that I don't have to do everything all by myself. I'm learning to have my students and colleagues help with classroom tasks. I'm learning to ask for help as opposed to getting stressed out, burnt out, and overwhelmed. In the process, I'm learning that sharing responsibilities is not only lightening my workload but also creating a supportive teaching-learning environment where everyone thrives.

Release Yourself from Blame

Resist the urge to blame yourself. Try not to beat up on yourself for things that might go wrong or for things that you have no control over. Recognize that you're human and not a machine. Work hard at developing resiliency. I'm not saying that we should call our friends over to celebrate what we consider failures. I'm encouraging us to recognize that things don't always go as planned. Even the best-planned lesson for the day that you're being evaluated on could be disrupted by students who are experiencing a mental health crisis. They may begin to display attention-seeking behaviors or may even be downright disruptive. Understand that we're all human beings, not robots, and neither are our students. Trauma manifests in multiple ways, including a lack of self-regulation. In those moments, go to your Plan B or C and celebrate the moments of success.

Questions for Your Journey

What's Your Baseline?

Beginning with oneself means acknowledging the knowledge gaps and skills limitations that you have in order to learn, grow, and thrive. Sometimes, it means becoming vulnerable, moving out of your comfort zone, and talking to people who are not in your circle of influence. It might mean giving up your seat at the table or acknowledging your own privilege, whether that privilege is race, class, or ethnic background. Offering help without understanding where traumatized kids are coming from only results in frustration, miscommunication, and broken trust. Once you know what you're missing, you can begin to fill in the gaps and then meet students where they are.

Meeting students where they are involves a commitment to ongoing learning. It requires a relentless pursuit of knowledge about systemic issues that are drivers of adverse childhood experiences. It means using a trauma-informed lens and leaving all preconceived judgments and biases at the door.

As a classroom teacher, I make a concerted effort to read as many articles on trauma-informed practices as time permits, allowing me to stay informed about the insights and recommendations put forth by professionals and experts in the field. Listen, all of us have biases, and unlearning can become quite an endeavor. However, I encourage all of us to be patient. As the old saying goes, "Rome was not built in a day." With time and dedication, and a commitment to equity and creating trauma-informed schools, we will make the grade.

I remained haunted by Carol's words—"Marcia, I feel like such a failure, a loser!"—and I had a deep desire to help. This is where the trauma-informed practices survey I put together came in. I wanted to get a better idea of where teachers were starting from, so I could see what kind of help was needed.

Consider the second question on the survey: "Was trauma or trauma-informed practices a part of your teacher preparation program?" Most of the respondents didn't hear about trauma or trauma-informed practices in their teacher preparation programs. Here were some of their responses.

- "I did not actively engage in trauma-informed practices until I enrolled in an elective course titled 'urban education.'"

- "It must have been mentioned in my education class at some point, but I don't exactly remember. It's been a while."

- "Trauma/trauma-informed practices were not in my teacher education program. I have had one PD session on trauma/trauma-informed practices—it was great, but nothing before that."

- "I learned it from you."

- "I did not learn anything at all about trauma and children in my teacher education programs. I only learned about it when I was already a teacher and I engaged in some workshops."

Of all the respondents to my survey, only one participant noted that the issue of trauma and trauma-informed teaching was included in their teacher education program. That participant, let me make haste to say, attended a private institution. How disconnected is all of this from reality? How can educators be expected to help children dealing with ACEs if the education and training they receive never addresses this specific issue?

The responses spoke directly to what Carol was feeling. She, like many of the respondents, was simply unprepared to work with children who had seen and experienced devastation and trauma in their young lives. I don't believe that the majority of teachers don't care; they do. They simply lack the knowledge and skill set necessary to deal with the bombardment of behaviors brought on by trauma.

So, what can teachers and school personnel do? Firstly, I recommend that educators not beat up on themselves or others. As teachers, there are already tons of people beating up on us already—don't join them! Secondly, there's so much more valuable information out there now than when I went to college, and I bet you could say the same. Lean on your colleagues, collaborate by sharing articles or perhaps hosting a book club on one of the books from the Resources section. Engage in open dialogue about the challenges you're facing and make time to explore case studies to find effective ways to manage classroom disruptions.

Too often I've witnessed educators vent their frustrations about students' behaviors, target particular students, and speak about kids in an almost detrimental manner. That isn't helpful. While sharing pertinent information about students can be valuable, it should be done in a way that doesn't harbor negative biases or judgments toward students. Call upon your own humanity when dealing with traumatized children, be proactive, and educate yourself.

Case in point, Kristy had been an elementary school teacher for fifteen years. She had no formal training in trauma-informed teaching but allowed her instincts from being a mother to guide the way she interacted with her students. "All children need to be cared for," she said. "They are no different from my own kids at home."

Kristy is mindful that the fourth-graders in her class live in poverty in the urban core and experience traumatic events in their lives. She comes to school every day with the mindset that she'll be loving and fair, but firm. She makes sure she sets daily expectations that each person in the class community adheres to. She incorporates SEL in every aspect of her daily routine, including recess. She explicitly teaches her students modes of behavior in and out of the classroom while modeling what she wants them to emulate. Overall, she's proactive as opposed to waiting for disruptive behaviors to occur.

Finally, discuss with your district leaders or school administrators the need for carefully designed, culturally responsive, trauma-informed professional development training that will enhance your effectiveness. If this isn't an option or isn't approved for some reason, be that change! Danica, who works at a public school in an urban area, reported on the survey that she first learned about the term "trauma-informed" three or four years ago when colleagues began an initiative to increase awareness of the effects of student trauma. In that case, it was the teachers who took the initiative to bring trauma-informed education and practices to their school. You too can be that change.

What's Your Lived Experience?

When my twin boys, Eric and Terrence, were around six or seven, my husband, our other kids, and I went on a road trip in our eight-seater passenger van. We were driving to Virginia to see my older sister and to spend a week enjoying nature out of the city. While we were talking about what we would do, Terrence blurted out, "All my teachers live in the woods."

Terrence went on to graduate from a four-year college, but years later, I still haven't forgotten his words. In the way of children, he shared a simple, honest truth: most teachers who teach in my city, and in cities all over the States, don't live in the same community where they work. This means that they aren't always able to identify or connect to the lived experiences of the majority of students they teach. As I've discussed previously, living in the same city or town as your students is highly beneficial because you have first-hand exposure to the issues that your students face, an ability to attend the same events your students might engage in, and an opportunity to interact with students' families in the community. The advantages of living within proximity to your students' lives are immeasurable.

While having lived experiences similar to those of your students can be beneficial, it's neither a guarantee that students will have a positive experience in class, nor a requirement for trauma-informed teaching. I've observed teachers build loving, trusting professional relationships with students with whom they have absolutely nothing in common.

Take Debbie, for example, a white teacher who has taught in city schools in Chicago. She was raised in what she describes as a super loving home where her parents made sure she was exposed to the arts and sciences, and that she had opportunities to study after school as opposed to working. For her senior year in college, she was part of a study abroad program, so she also had the opportunity to explore the world. These are the hallmarks of a middle-class life, which meant that she had no idea that American students lived in deep poverty until she got a job in a Chicago school. As opposed to her middle-class schooling, most of the children she encountered in her new job were Black and brown, and received free lunch. The first thing she said she did was let her students know her background; she explained it to them, not to make them feel badly about their own situations in life but because she wanted to begin her teaching career with trust and transparency. It was also an opportunity to find out what she and her students have in common. Some could connect with her love of animals, others with her love of art. She used these commonalities to begin relationships. At the beginning of the first year, however, the kids didn't trust her, but she worked really hard to develop relationships with each of them—even the kids that other teachers told her were hard to reach. This recognition of the need to foster student-teacher relationships is key to being a trauma-informed educator.

Debbie also had to recognize that though she had an easy and enriching school experience, not all of her students were afforded that opportunity. She had to acknowledge that although the curriculum was intended to be fast-paced, she needed to find ways to make it accessible to the variety of needs of her tenth-grade students. Her class included multilingual learners, newcomers from other countries, regular education students, and special education students. Therefore, she took her diverse student population into account when planning and executing her lessons in order to maximize growth potential. She incorporated brain breaks and varied hands-on instruction that would get them out from behind their screens for portions of her class. Where Debbie's high school education included many hands-on experiences provided by her family, she knew that she would have to be the one to expose her students to real-world projects that would engage and enrich all of her students, even those whose parents couldn't send them to museums and science camps.

This is why Debbie employed project-based learning. For many students, the project-based activities were a big hit. Kids loved getting out of their seats, moving around the classroom, joking, and having lots of fun while still learning. Personally, I like project-based work because it provides opportunities for kids to use multiple intelligences. Lessons like these are not pigeonholed to focus on a particular learning style but instead consider the entire learning spectrum. Of course, this may require more time planning and implementing, but it's worth the effort and benefits students who are more likely to engage in non-traditional modes of teaching and learning.

Planning non-traditional lessons can sometimes be difficult

for teachers who were often, traditionally, the best students, but it's important to remember that effective teachers are those who go outside of their lived experience to bring teaching and learning to life. My recommendation is that, if you're a teacher, administrator, related services provider, or paraprofessional and you have zero idea of what it is to live a traumatic life, don't blame yourself. It's not your fault that you grew up in privilege. It's not your fault that you weren't exposed to adverse childhood experiences. If you are that privileged teacher, however, your job is to educate yourself about ACEs, trauma, and their effects on children.

Talk to teachers who are compassionate and who might have had the students prior to you getting them. Learn how to respond to students' social and academic needs. Stay away from teachers who harbor pessimism and have nothing flattering to say about kids. Be the voice demanding ongoing professional development training on how to best connect and respond to children who may have different lived experiences than yourself. Debbie's story illustrates how intentional this teacher was in learning, growing, and thriving right along with her students. With so many children limited in their opportunities to get outside of their communities, may we strive to be for our students what Debbie was to hers.

Why Does Representation Matter?

The more appropriate question should be: "Why doesn't representation matter?" Representation matters because it gives children and their families a sense of belonging. To walk into a school and see folks who look like you, speak your language, and with whom you can identify with automatically increases your sense of safety and belonging.

To give an example, the fact that I am Jamaican made a difference in the life of my student, Kevon. He was new to our school, beginning well into the second quarter. It wasn't long before we found each other, and when I smiled at Kevon in the hallways, his beautiful face lit up, greeting me with "Whey ah gwan?"

"Nutten nah gwan," came my instantaneous response. Kevon knew that he could say hello in the Jamaican dialect. This allowed him to feel a sense of belonging, and because of our shared experience, he sought me out for support when he was unsure of how to negotiate school.

Representation isn't simply a pedagogical approach. It's the lifeblood of classroom spaces where children are seen, valued, and empowered. It's where children see models whom they can identify with in more ways than just language.

Representation serves as a cornerstone for cultivating a sense of identity and empowerment. For students, especially Black, brown, newcomers to the US, kids in foster care, and non-binary students, inclusive representation goes beyond visibility. It serves as a powerful catalyst for creating the next generation of educators and leaders.

This issue is very important to me because, like our students, I've been in situations where my lived experience has been vastly different from those with whom I am learning. I was an adult attending college for my graduate degree, and in all of my classes except one did I have a person who looked like me. I didn't feel like I belonged. This lack of representation made me feel invisible, although I knew I wasn't. It was also clear that those I went to school with had no idea how to interact with me, an "other." No one spoke to me, although I was capable of speaking entirely in English. Whenever there were conversations and I chimed in, the response was silence. I didn't feel safe, and neither did I feel like I belonged. It was in those moments that I recommitted myself to teaching inclusion of all people, all experiences, and all voices.

Along with this, I still believe it's crucial to recruit and train qualified teachers and other support staff whose race, gender (including transgender and non-binary people), background, and ethnicity match those of the student population. There must be representation in special education and social work departments that aren't predominantly white. In addition, local education agencies must commit to having representation at every level. There must be representation at school boards, school committees, and in school administration.

Another important element of representation that must not be overlooked is the ability to learn from each other. We are in the midst of the process of globalization, and learning about cultures and being appreciative of cultures that are foreign to us is such a beautiful gift. To learn about other people's culture and language, and to read the books that they read and vice versa is wonderful. As a teacher who's experienced so much trauma in my own life, to be able to teach children who live in and with community violence gives me the opportunity to encourage and help kids overcome some of those barriers.

I wish I had the opportunity to show off my country, my "language," and the amazing qualities that Jamaica offers in my graduate classes. I didn't, and that was a loss for all of the other students in my classes. I would have also loved the opportunity to learn about the dominant culture at the time. So, as you can see, representation matters, and not just to new arrivals or people from other races, ethnic backgrounds, or gender. It matters to all of us.

Helpful Hints from Teachers

- *Always have a solid plan of activities and alternative options*, including a back-up plan for those days when things just don't happen as expected. This is especially true for days when you're going to be evaluated.

- *Don't take work home.*

- *Know that the kids who act up the most are usually the ones who need the most love, care, and attention.*

- *Take breaks when you need them.* Don't wait until you're overwhelmed. Make a pact with your co-teacher or other colleagues that you will ask each other for help when you need a five-minute break.

- *Include room in your lessons for different voices and languages.* Find books, articles, poems, and videos created by authors that represent your students. Allow time for students to share and celebrate their cultures.

CHAPTER 9

STRATEGIES FOR LISTENING

IT WAS ALMOST the end of the school year and grades were due in three days. Erica needed to complete the end-of-unit assessment, which I kept telling her would boost her grade and take her from the failing column. She kept dodging me. When we finally met, she told me that she didn't care if she failed the quarter or not. I dug deeper, wanting to learn more since she'd previously been deeply invested in earning good grades.

"I honestly don't want to pass English," Erica said.

"Why? I know you can do it, and you know you can do it, too."

"Because I'm moving to another school, and I really don't care," she snapped back. "Miss, I've told you this so many times. I don't care, and you're not listening to me."

Then she clammed up and refused to speak. I began to think about my actions over the week or so following our conversation. Erica was right. I wasn't listening. I wasn't taking what she was saying into consideration. I kept pushing for a desired response or action. I was focused on what I thought was good for her in terms of passing the class.

In hindsight, I should have responded to her feelings about moving to another school. Her fear of moving out of state and leaving her friends behind. That was a lot for a child. Often, children become displaced and move from school to school, which makes it hard for them to feel comfortable building and sustaining friendships, and feel a sense of belonging.

If I could have that conversation again, I would praise Erica for the work she'd done over the last quarter, actively listen to what she said, and try to assure her that I understood her concerns. Connecting her to the school social worker, who could help make sure she had a smooth transition, could be my next course of action. As you can see, I'm still learning and growing.

Perhaps the most important skill a trauma-informed teacher can have is listening to understand. Truly and actively listening to what children are saying—and what they are not saying—is a huge guiding force in how I try to approach difficult situations. On the other side of the coin, knowing how to talk so that kids listen is just as important. It doesn't matter how stunningly brilliant or full of good intentions our words are; if kids don't want to listen, they won't take in any of it. In this chapter, I'll make a case for the power of listening and how it should be a shared power between teachers and students.

Listening to Kids Talk

It was my final day at the high school where I'd worked as a special education teacher for six years. As I stood in the hallway, taking a moment to reflect on my time at the school, Mr. Ryan, another teacher, came over to chat.

"Mrs. Ranglin-Vassell, I'm going to miss you. Your leaving will be a huge loss to the school."

Between trying to compose myself and wanting to pretend that I wasn't a softy, I mustered up the strength to ask him why he said those words to me. What he shared in response opened the floodgates of tears.

"You're patient with kids. You let them talk, and you let them say everything they have to say without interrupting them. Then when you say a word or two, you show them alternatives to their behaviors that make them feel safe. You are not judgmental, and I like that."

His words still make my heart glow. I think it's very important that teachers connect with each other. Not just in a transactional way but in ways to share and support each other. This is important in community building. The same can be said for how teachers and students connect. I find it disheartening that there isn't more focus on cultivating the teacher-student bond. Most of the hours we spend with kids are meant to be used for instruction, but that's not the way to build relationships and truly connect with kids.

Knowing that adults listen to them is important for kids. It's an especially big deal for traumatized children, who often find it challenging to develop bonds and form attachments in ways that open them up to meaningful conversations. Building trust requires a lot of time and patience. Children who experience betrayal from adults, siblings, or a system that was meant to protect them find it difficult to open up. I make it a point not to pry or force my students into sharing details about their lives unless, of course, they choose to do so voluntarily. I pay close attention to students and reassure them that I'm here if they ever wish to share their thoughts and concerns in private.

I'm not the only one who approaches listening in this way. My friend, Jill Baker, is a highly effective teacher with twenty-seven years of experience, and she understands the importance of listening so kids talk. Jill's first step is to take them out of the classroom and to a confidential space. She tells them that she's there to listen to them. During the conversations, she actively listens, uses body language like eye contact and nodding her head, and only interjects occasionally to affirm the child.

In cases where kids are in a crisis and may pose a threat to themselves or others, Jill involves the school psychologist, social worker, and administration for help. Before bringing anyone in to help, she explains, in a comforting and calm tone, what it means to be a mandatory reporter. This way, the kids don't feel that she has betrayed their confidence. Even after referrals, Jill continues to support the kids, including by visiting their homes if necessary.

Another teacher who leads by listening is Mr. Abdullah, and his example offers a window into a great listening technique. Carla was a beautiful fifth grader with a sunny disposition. But one day, she walked into the classroom and appeared upset, her face marked with tears, and hyperventilating. Mr. Abdullah noticed her distress and took her aside to ask her what the issue was. She didn't answer. Mr. Abdullah told her that he was sorry that she was upset, encouraged her to relax, and asked her if she wanted to either sit on the comfy chair in the reading area or if she wanted to go and speak to the social worker. She didn't respond but went over to the reading area.

Mr. Abdullah got the rest of the class working on their worksheets and went to check on Carla. He noticed that she was a bit more relaxed but had started to shed silent tears. Mr. Abdullah encouraged Carla to do some belly breathing, going through a few rounds with her. Reluctantly, she followed his advice and soon appeared calmer. She was able to join the rest of the class and finish the assignment.

Later, Carla asked Mr. Abdullah if she could talk to him.

Mr. Abdullah had a profound understanding of listening so kids will talk. His strategy was simple. First, he would put the whole teacher thing aside and treat kids as human beings—not robots, not miniature adults, but human beings with thoughts, feelings, and emotions of their own. Human beings who have a voice as well as agency. Students need to know that they can trust you and that you won't let them down. When it was clear that Carla wasn't willing or able to talk in the moment of her distress, Mr. Abdullah didn't pressure her. Instead, he gave Carla the space and time to process her emotions. He gave her options: go and try to relax in the reading area or go to see the social worker. Then, he respected her choice, letting her process things while making sure she knew he was available.

For kids who experience trauma, it becomes difficult to believe or trust adults. They have been let down and felt the sting of disappointment so many times that they have developed a self-protection that manifests as a basic lack of trust for adults or authority. Mr. Abdullah says it's important not to personalize it. Their actions are not about you or anyone else. It's about a young person protecting their hearts from hurt or betrayal. Even if they're yelling and screaming profanities—it isn't about you. Mr. Abdullah says, "Let them scream. You won't go to hell for that." Instead, focus on actively listening to what they do want to share. Unless you have a solid relationship with a child, you should not try to ask too many questions and only show real concern and empathy.

In addition, when kids are talking to you, give them your full attention. Don't let them down by checking your phone or by texting. If you don't have the time to give 100 percent, let your young person know and ask if it's something that can wait until you can give them your undivided attention.

What If They Won't Talk?

Sometimes, getting kids who are experiencing trauma to talk can be difficult. They may be overwhelmed by their emotions and unable to express themselves verbally. They may be used to no one listening to them or considering their opinions. Whatever the case may be, sometimes listening well means asking the right questions.

I recall getting into big fights with Jen, a high schooler, every Friday when we had to walk down to the library from the Bridge School. It wasn't a long walk, and I looked forward to getting out in the fresh air. Not Jen. This normally quiet and respectful student would flip out, cursing and swearing every time we had to walk down the street. I couldn't figure it out until I asked the big question—*why?* We were just about to leave the classroom when Jen had another outburst, refusing to leave while all the other kids filed out. Instead of reprimanding her or demanding that she get back in line, I took her aside, waited for her to calm down, and just said, "Why don't you want to go on this walk to the library?"

Jen told me that her mother had been prostituting herself at the bus stop—the one we walked right by on the way to the library. She was embarrassed by the sex work and sexual exploitation that her mother had to endure, and even more ashamed that her mom only did it to keep the roof over their heads. Her mom also suffered from drug addiction, and Jen had been living in a group home as a ward of the state. She wasn't having an easy time. I still remember vividly the pain in Jen's eyes, the trembling, the sweating, and the pacing around the tiny classroom. I held Jen close to me, letting her tears roll mercilessly down my blouse. I didn't care. The only thing that mattered was Jen, her feelings, her emotions.

That was the last time Jen ever went to the library. Instead, I'd check books out and make sure she had what she needed to study at the school or to take home for leisure reading. I wasn't going to inflict more pain and trauma on this child. I made every effort to talk to Jen more, love her more, and care for her even more. Jen wasn't a bad kid, but she was a victim of bad circumstances who was experiencing lots of secondary trauma and trauma memories.

Through this, I learned the importance of simply asking *why*. I learned to listen with non-judgmental ears, and after that, Jen and I became like two peas in a pod. All because I had taken the time to ask *why* and truly listen to her when she told me what was wrong. Educators must go the extra mile to compassionately provide help and support when students confide in them.

Whoever said, "Kids must be seen and not heard," must not have thought that children are real people with emotions, thoughts, and agency. Trust is everything. You don't talk to folks you don't trust, so why should kids? Also, children are quite intuitive—traumatized kids, even more so. Their antennas are always up, and they are constantly on high alert. They read body language legibly, so check in with your body language meter and see how you're doing.

I've never taught a child I didn't love. Yes, there have been kids who have gotten under my skin and have irritated me. But instead of getting mad at them or saying mean things about them to others, I get curious. Why are they acting that way? What would make them feel more comfortable and able to share their needs? Kids need compassion, and I try to approach teaching with lots of it.

Teaching and learning can be exhausting, and with all the traumatic events globally, it doesn't hurt to let students know that they are appreciated and loved. In fact, everyone wants to hear that they are loved, so I make it a practice to say, "I love you" to students. Sometimes, I get blank stares, or they look at me like I'm some unidentifiable object from Mars. Other times, they will light up or even say, "I love you too, Miss." Whatever their response, it's okay. The important thing is saying it and meaning it. Saying "I love you" humanizes teacher-student relationships and lets children know how valued they are to you.

Talking So Kids Listen

My grandmother Lillian was hilarious. She always had a story to tell: a proverb or a parable. In moments when I'm unsure of what to say or do, I channel the wisdom of my grandmother. When my siblings and I became too "chatterboxy," she would quietly chime in using the rich Jamaican patois, "God give oonu two ears an' one mout', it mean yuh must listen twice as much as oonu talk." Those words continue to help me today in my role as a teacher. Because I want my students to listen to me, I make a conscious effort to listen to them. And I try not to talk over my students.

If I'm presenting a lesson and they become boisterous or too loud, I stop the lesson and say, "When I'm speaking, you're listening; when you're speaking, I'm listening." That usually quiets the room and gives me an opportunity to continue direct instruction. Then I follow through on that promise, making sure I make space for their voices to be heard. This may mean quieting the room so that students can respond to a class question without interruption or momentarily leaving the room to actively listen to a student who needs to speak to me privately. For me, it's all about respect and empathy in the classroom, allowing students to use their voices and have that agency to be who they are without feeling afraid of negative repercussions.

I'm not the kind of teacher who yells and screams. I learned a long time ago that the minute you begin to yell, you've already lost the battle. (Some days, teaching goes as planned, while other times, it's like you're in a war zone—something I say with affection!) The case against yelling is based on the fact that you can't always know what a child is dealing with. There may be yelling and screaming already in their houses, so why would you then want to replicate that in your classroom?

Here's an example of how to talk so kids listen: Ray and Keith had been friends since middle school; they worked well together and would often joke and play around. Play for them could sometimes include jokingly poking or even slapping each other. Their teachers would occasionally notice these behaviors and would redirect them, which usually worked. Ray and Keith were a good team and supported each other. They consistently earned good grades.

But one day, things took an unexpected turn. The two had been playing and horsing around, but Ray stopped because he wanted to focus on his classwork. Keith didn't realize and playfully slapped Ray on the head. Rather than retaliating or asking his friend to stop, Ray stormed out of the classroom, venting his frustration by punching every locker that was in his sight. As there was another teacher in the classroom, I followed Ray and asked him to tell me his side of the story.

After actively listening, I told him how sorry I was that he and his friend had a falling out. I told him how much I admired their friendship and how much I appreciated the way they worked together. Using lots of "I" messages, I told Ray that I knew how much he valued the friendship that he and Keith had and that I thought it was a good idea to explain to Keith the way he felt.

Separately, I had a similar conversation with Keith, sharing that he could explain to Ray that he was sorry about what happened and that he'd thought they were still playing. I made sure I was non-judgmental as we talked. This didn't mean that I couldn't turn this into a learning experience. I gently reminded him of the times the teachers had asked him and Ray to stop horsing around because they didn't want anyone to get hurt. After our conversation, Keith told me that he was sorry about what happened, but he was not ready to talk to Ray. I assured him that there was no rush but encouraged him to have the conversation as soon as he felt like it. The following day, he did just that. I was thrilled to see the pair back to their old selves again.

This was just a small conflict, but its resolution hinges on listening. First, I listened to the boys, and then I had a conversation with them—not reprimanding or demanding anything, just talking through what happened. Because of the good relationships I'd already established with them, this was easy.

Below are great examples of some factors that I've found crucial for conflict resolution:

- *Private Conversation.* I didn't address the concerns in the classroom where all the students were present and instruction was going on. Instead, I stepped out of the classroom for a private conversation. If you're a regular education teacher and don't have a co-teacher to lean on, pick up the phone and call an administrator to cover your class for a few minutes while you have a quick conversation with students. Removing the students from the classroom prevents triggers and respects the time of the other students.

- *Active Listening.* I actively listened to each boy's account of what occurred. I remained present throughout our time together, providing affirmations, focusing on each account, reflecting on their respective accounts, and providing verbal and non-verbal cues, such as nodding and maintaining eye contact.

- *Empathetic Speaking.* When it was my turn to talk, I ensured that my tone was soft and empathetic throughout the conversation. That way, I could convey that my intention was to help mend fences, not to assign blame or judgment. It was also important for me to let the students know that I valued their friendship and collaboration and genuinely cared about each of them. I also offered some light advice without telling them to stop their playful habit or change anything. I simply asked them if they thought the playful slapping might be getting in the way of their friendship and their studies.

- *Respectful Timing.* I respected Keith's decision not to speak to Ray immediately. Instead of rushing him, I welcomed his willingness to have the conversation, while emphasizing the need to eventually address the issue.

In this way, I could act as a moderator for the boys, simply helping them regulate strong emotions, guiding them in self-reflection, and offering suggestions for next steps. These are all hallmarks of Social-Emotional Learning and part of effective trauma-informed teaching. Letting students have agency over their choices is a great way to get them to care more about the outcome. Giving the students control over the situation also helps them understand how to make better decisions in the future.

Sometimes, talking so kids listen doesn't even need to include talking. Let me explain. Michael was one of my students, and though I knew he'd experienced a traumatic situation, that was all the information I had. Of course, that could mean a myriad of things, and the way Michael reacted to teacher interaction varied. The seemingly happy child who was always volunteering to read in class had suddenly become what some of his teachers were calling a "pain in the ass." He wasn't listening and was moving uncontrollably and disruptively around his small classroom. I'd tried everything that I thought I had in my toolkit. Nothing worked. I felt like such a failure until, one day, I decided that I would write Michael a letter.

> *"Dear Michael," I began. "You have been such an amazing*
> *student. I love when you read in class. You have been doing*
> *so great, but I know now that you've missed several assign-*
> *ments. Please let me help you to make the work up. I am here*
> *after school, please let me help you."*

I gave Michael the handwritten letter. He had the biggest smile on his face. With the advent of social media, we don't do as many handwritten notes and letters. I try to do them as much as possible. Even children who have grown up with computers and the internet understand the time and energy that goes into handwritten letters. Receiving one makes them feel special and seen. For the next several days, Michael cooperated and did his work. He wasn't immediately perfect, but he calmed down and tried hard to get back on track. I don't think for one minute that what happened in the scenario was magic. It was all about stepping outside of the box to figure out a solution to a behavior that wasn't simply disruptive to the class community but one in which the child was inhibiting his own growth. By writing to be heard, I demonstrated that I was listening to my students' needs.

Listening is a huge part of what we do as educators. Finding strategies that work for you to really listen to kids will grow your relationships with them and help them see you as someone who has their best interests at heart. The more you can strengthen that bond, the more you can discover who they are as people and what they need to thrive.

Helpful Hints for Teachers

- *When kids act up, let curiosity be your first response.* Ask *why* and listen to the answer.

- *Remind yourself that some things are out of your control* and they aren't worth worrying about. Let those things go so you can focus your energy on what you can change.

- *Practice gratitude.* At the end of the day, write down a list of five things that you are grateful for. By noticing the positive in your life, you will be better able to notice the positive in others.

- *Practice active listening in other ways.* When was the last time you sat and truly listened to a song from start to finish without multitasking or thinking about something else? Try taking a walk and tuning into your sense of sound. What do you hear?

- *Praise more than you criticize.* Think of students as a bank. You must deposit a lot of positivity before you can make a withdrawal in the form of correction.

CHAPTER 10

SELF-CARE FOR EDUCATORS

I KNOW YOU might be on the edge of skipping this chapter, but don't stop reading! This chapter is undoubtedly the most important of this book. Why? Well, though I've been in education actively teaching kids for decades, no one ever sat me down and emphasized the importance of self-care. Yes, I've talked to others about how exhausting the life of a teacher can be, but it always seems to end with a "Well, what can you do?" kind of attitude. Though we are tired, we can't afford to not give each interaction, each lesson, each day our all.

I've come to the realization that I must take care of myself before I can effectively take care of others. We simply cannot pour from an empty cup! So please, take the time to read this chapter and take the ideas to heart. The suggestions and insights in this chapter have been gathered from talking to educators all across the spectrum. Find what works for you. It's my hope that you take something from this chapter that helps you to continue experiencing joy and gratification in your job, even though it's not always the easiest.

You Are Worthy

As long as I live, I will hold Mrs. Killingly in my heart. A beautiful and intelligent teacher-librarian, she was the epitome of professionalism. She worked at a high school for decades and decades, doing everything in her power to support the students. In fact, she was a fixture in the library; it belonged to her. On my visits to her school, I would always make my way up to the library to see her. I enjoyed engaging in conversations that ranged from the lighthearted to the serious.

It was during one of our extensive conversations that she shared something profound with me.

"I'm not leaving this place," she said. "The hearse is going to have to take me out."

She said it with a grin, but I knew it was a testament to her mission as a librarian and to her students. Mrs. Killingly was determined to be a librarian for as long as she possibly could. Her words resounded in my soul like thunder. All of a sudden, I felt inept, as though I wasn't as good as she was. It took me a long time to realize that I couldn't compare myself to her. I had to force myself away from the negative self-talk and remind myself that I was an amazing teacher who cared deeply for my students. While I still admire her quiet strength and absolute dedication, I had other obligations, a family, and work in my community. I made a promise to myself that I wouldn't leave school in a Cadillac.

If we don't look out and care for ourselves, who will? If we don't care for our own physical, mental, and emotional health, who will? Being an educator is just another way to say you are a caregiver, and caregivers notoriously neglect their own well-being, placing their health on the back burner of life. I've shown up at work with more than one injury or illness, convinced that I needed to be there for my kids. I'm not alone in this. Other teachers have soldiered on while being sick, feeling guilty for taking even one day off to recover. We don't want to let our kids, our co-teachers, or our team down. Teaching may be the only profession whereby teachers feel as if they have committed a mortal sin for taking a sick day. For me, whether it was cluster migraines, a cracked vertebra (more on that in a minute), or a persistent cough, I was *not* going to be absent.

But I have a new perspective on this now. My new mantra around this is, "These kids deserve my best. If I can't give my best today, I shouldn't be there at all." Of course, it's not always that black and white, so the idea is to check in with yourself. Are you able to give your best today? Or do you need space to heal?

And this doesn't just apply to when you are physically sick. Let us commit, together, to normalizing taking a sick day or mental health day if we need it. The sky isn't falling; your students will be taken care of while you recover. Being at your best means that you can give them your best.

Of course, I'm guilty of overlooking these things and even looking down on them as unimportant. But I've learned some valuable lessons. In 2018, I fell and cracked one of my vertebrae. I was out of work for a few months and could hardly walk without feeling pain. Despite the excruciating pain, it was difficult for me to detach from the activities and routines of school. While I was lying in bed, I would mentally be going through periods one to seven, all of it. I wondered what the kids were doing, what conversations were happening in school, how so-and-so was getting along. I was texting everyone and worrying constantly—which didn't do anything to help me get better. Though I wasn't fully recovered, I went back to work. It was clear to everyone but me that I wasn't up to full capacity and was in obvious pain. My injury ended up dragging on much longer than it needed to, all because I wouldn't give my body the time it needed to heal. Therefore, my advice is simple: take care of yourself. *You matter.*

I can't help but think of my sister, Val, an extraordinary teacher, my role model, my guiding star, and friend. She nurtured countless gardens of knowledge, yet amid her dedication to others, her own health and well-being often took a backseat. I lost Val to breast cancer on December 1, 2022. I'm still at a loss that my shero, my sister, whom I love and admire, the person who I wanted to be just like, has passed away. Once in a while, I will pick up the phone to dial her and realize she isn't here with me. I still can't believe that she went home to Heaven so prematurely.

My sister began her teaching career in Kingston, Jamaica, and she always called her students her "stars." Despite her diagnosis, she continued to work until just a few months before she passed away. She loved her career, and she loved those kids. But I do wish that my sister had prioritized self-care a bit more. As I contemplate her path, and my own, I will learn the lessons my sister continues to teach. I see that there was room for her to give more of herself to herself. It's my commitment to give more to myself by practicing more self-compassion.

I share this story in part because if you are struggling to see yourself as worthy of your own time and attention, then do it for someone else. I miss Val every day. She was my biggest cheerleader and support. Now, I have to become my own biggest cheerleader.

As teachers, we must, without guilt or reservation, begin to see ourselves as worthy of self-care, worthy of being treated as professionals, and worthy of looking in the mirror and not being judgmental about prioritizing our health and well-being.

That sentence is worth reading again. Go ahead, I'll wait.

During trauma and loss, we tend to ignore our own needs. While I was devastated by Val's death, after my mom passed away, I truly fell into a dark place. I wasn't making the space to care for myself and had fallen out of my routines, which only made me feel worse. On top of that, I was feeling guilty for how little I felt that I was accomplishing because I was so tired, sad, and lost.

One morning as I gazed into the mirror, I was startled to see the reflection of my mother gazing back at me. I heard my mother's voice, clear and resounding, "Mar, yuh worthy of loving yuhself, yuh worthy of yuh own love, the same love and dedication yuh pour into others. Pour sum ah dat into yuhself."

That message seeped deep into my psyche. It was from Mom, said directly in the Jamaican dialect. I took action by reaching out to a mental health counselor. I began to prioritize my physical health and emotional well-being. I got back on a regular sleep schedule, which allowed me to get up at five in the morning to make a fresh salad for lunch and pray before school. I started feeling better, more like myself. And the more myself I felt, the more I was able to fully give myself to my students and other responsibilities. I'm so thankful that my mother arrived with that wake-up call.

Self-care is not one-and-done. It has to become a way of life, a conscious decision we must commit to as educators.

Physical Well-Being: Don't Go Out in a Black Cadillac

To honor and carry on the legacy of my sister and listen to the message my mom sent me, I vow to take care of myself. One way that I do that is by making sure to schedule and get my annual mammogram. Breast cancer runs in my family, so I'm definitely not taking any chances. This is because physical health is so important, and focusing on physical health is so vital to your success in the classroom.

Staying connected with your body is also a great way to help you determine when you are stressed. For me, the signals are migraine headaches that leave me feeling like I've been run over by an eighteen-wheeler, my introverted nature going into overdrive, and insomnia. What are yours? Once you clue into the physical effects of stress, you must find ways to address those very real physical effects. To illustrate, I walked into the teacher's room one afternoon to see Ariana, a thirty-something mother of three and a deeply devoted special education teacher, down on the floor doing push-ups. After I watched her do about fifteen in quick succession, she got up, breathing heavily.

"What was that all about?" I asked.

"It's just a simple way to decompress, and I like them a lot," she quipped. "Push-ups get me out of my head, and as an added bonus, I'm getting a lot stronger!"

Unchecked stress can kill you. As educators, it's important that we recognize our stress and make a conscious effort not to let it impede our responsibilities at work or our relationships. Though push-ups aren't for me, I really admire Ariana and her self-awareness. When she's feeling the pressures of the job, she gives herself the grace of a set of push-ups, allowing the stress to quickly move out of her body.

There's a clear link between your physical being and your mental health. I've shared how Ariana and I maintain physical health, but here are some more ways you can care for your physical body:

- *Get regular medical and dental exams.* Get blood work, mammograms, and other preventative tests to catch health issues early.

- *Stay home when you are sick.* You are not doing yourself, your students, and your colleagues a favor by coming in feeling poorly.

- *Set a sleep schedule and stick to it.* It can be helpful to set a reminder or alarm so that you have time to wind down.

- *Find ways to build movement into your day.* It doesn't have to be formal exercise, but plenty of studies have shown that moving our bodies is good for us. Whether that means taking the stairs, parking at the other end of the parking lot, or anything else, get creative about how you can add natural movement into your daily routine.

- *Try breathwork to calm your nervous system.* A nice practice is to take two minutes to simply sit and breathe at the end of the day once all the students have left. For those two minutes, focus on each breath and let go of any other thoughts. Breathe in deeply and slowly, breathe out deeply and slowly.

Emotional Well-Being: Filling Your Cup

Educators must also learn what the signals of burnout look like. Then, the number one thing to cope with stress is to continually fill your own cup. I've consciously developed a set of restorative strategies that I've found helpful over time. Every morning, I get myself out of bed and practice guided meditation coupled with prayer, a conversation asking God to guide my steps, seeking guidance for my journey and wisdom as I work to advance peace, love, and justice. Then, I spend some time stretching my body and speaking positive self-affirmations into my life.

If you know me at all, you also know that I love to walk, dance, cook, and journal. Cooking has also provided me with solace and peace. Whenever I'm stressed out or annoyed by situations that I have no control over, I cook. It's everything about cooking Jamaican cuisine that soothes my soul and enriches me for the next day. The preparation of the meal, the chopping of the veggies, the smell and the public display on social media of my veggie soup or whatever I make brings me joy, balance, and resilience as well as fuel for the next fight.

In the past, I've also sought mental health support, and teachers at all experience levels owe it to themselves and their students to practice self-care.

I spent a few weeks randomly asking colleagues what they did to fill their cup. I noticed many of them chuckled before responding. When I asked why they laughed, the common thread was that no one had ever asked them that question before. As I delved deeper, I realized that self-care for educators was simply overlooked by school districts, building administrators, and educators themselves. We can do better. I encourage you to—no, I "demand" you—explore self-care practices that make sense to you in order to optimize your own wellness. When you are stressed out or you feel like you're losing control, do something that restores you and brings you joy. Here's a small list of things that you can do daily to protect your mental health, compiled from my own experience and suggestions from fellow educators.

This list is by no means exhaustive, but it's a great place to start:

- *Practice gratitude.* Sometimes, life comes at me with a vengeance. It seems that things are falling all over the darn place. In those moments, I have to remind myself to be grateful. Express gratitude for the people, things, and opportunities that you have in your life.

- *Celebrate and affirm.* Look in the mirror and affirm yourself. This can feel strange when you start doing it, but it makes a difference. Tell yourself, "I am beautiful.

I am worthy of love. I am an amazing educator." The goal is to fall in love with yourself every single day. This means you must also compliment yourself. This can be small, such as, "I make the best scrambled eggs." Take time to acknowledge—just to yourself—that you are excellent at so many things. Celebrate your successes, and let others celebrate you too.

- *Prioritize boundaries.* "No" might be one of the hardest words to say, especially to your own family and those you love, yet it's the most powerful tool in maintaining your health and well-being. Practicing the art of setting limits and saying "No" is the most transformative way of taking care of yourself. This means saying no without feeling guilty. If you struggle with saying no, have candid conversations about that with your colleagues, partner, and others. If others are aware of putting too much on your plate, they will be more selective in what they come to you for. It's also okay to ask someone for time to think about whether or not you can take on what they're asking.

- *Engage in mindful activities.* Find solace in activities that nurture your mind and spirit. This may be tending to a garden, strolling through and enjoying nature, embracing yoga's calming embrace, adding daily time for reflection, recognizing what you have control of and what you cannot control, engaging in invigorating exercise, cooking meals, and spicing it up with love, knitting, quilting, or crafting. In fact, you should do a fun activity for yourself at least once a week. It can be helpful to plan out this activity in advance. Take a bath, watch a movie, paint your nails, go hiking, fly a kite, enjoy live music, read a book outside. Experience life!

- *Express yourself.* Each day, set a timer for ten minutes and practice free writing. This means just putting pen to paper and writing. Let out everything on the page— no prompts, no editing, no judging. I find it especially useful in the evening, so I can go to bed without my worries and thoughts swirling around. Writing them down is a good way to remind yourself and to help you put things in perspective.

- *Forge connections.* Seek companionship and friendships by joining clubs or cultivating bonds with family or friends who offer unwavering support. Together, you can pursue opportunities that illuminate your path to joy and purpose.

Mental Well-Being: Remembering Your Why

At the tender age of six, I knew that I wanted to be a teacher. Nothing else. This seems to be a trend. All the teachers I surveyed were asked, "Why did you become a teacher?" And many responses included a variation of loving the profession, wanting to help children succeed, or having deep admiration for teachers as a child.

While many of us were inspired to be teachers in our youth, every teacher has their individual reason for entering education— and it's never because they thought they'd be rich! They want to help kids. But as with any activity, when you're in the trenches just trying to get everything checked off your list each day, it can be difficult to remember your Why—the reason you got yourself into this in the first place.

I just want to take this moment to really shine a light on teachers. I see you! I have the deepest respect and admiration for the work you do and the care you take with other people's children. I've seen many teachers spending their own money on food, clothes, haircuts, and other incidentals so children can come to school feeling confident and prepared. I've also seen teachers lining up at bookstores and stationery shops to spend their own money on charts, highlighters, pens, and whatever else they deem necessary in order to provide supplies that their schools won't provide.

In addition, teachers spend countless evenings and weekends doing unpaid work. An *Education Week* article stated, "It's not uncommon for teachers to clock in extra hours each day to ensure they meet students' academic and social-emotional needs. But everything from answering emails to grading papers adds up: A typical teacher works about fifty-four hours a week—with just under half of that time devoted to directly teaching students." Historically, it was not unusual for me to work sixty to seventy hours per week with additional hours outside of the school day and at home. The point is that teachers clearly have a high level of commitment, not just for the profession but for the children they teach. But we need to acknowledge that stress is an inevitable part of this job and budget for it.

Teachers are at high risk for overwork and burnout, and when we encounter these issues, we forget our Why. It becomes easier to dehumanize the students and others around you, and you may begin to feel that you simply need to get through the day. If you find yourself feeling angry, wanting to yell at your students, or saying mean things about them in your mind or to your colleagues, your cup is empty. You've lost sight of your Why.

Follow up with yourself and your colleagues if you notice this happening to them. *Where did that anger come from? Why am I feeling this way—was it a certain incident or just pent-up stress?* Once you have determined why you are feeling that way, then try some of the following strategies to pull yourself out of a frustrated mindset and maintain your Why:

- *Focus on your Why each day.* By remembering that you have a greater purpose and that every action you take can be a step toward that goal, it's easier to let go of passing negative thoughts and frustrations. Take some time to write out your Why on a piece of paper. It could be the reason that inspired you to become a teacher, a specific student who you helped and remember fondly, or a larger goal for yourself or your school. When you are having a moment of frustration, pull out your piece of paper and tell yourself: *This moment is just a small bump in the road.* Then, read your Why and let it fill you up.

- *Detoxify your surroundings.* Surround yourself with joyful and uplifting energy. This can be through items that bring you joy, but the surest way to do this is to align yourself with positive and happy people. Stay clear of toxic people and individuals. Spend time with folks who see the bright side of things instead of those who are professional complainers. The latter can be emotionally draining and are unlikely to fill your heart and lift your spirits. You might want to spend time with them to try to change their mind, but don't get bogged down. They will suck the life out of you like a vampire (My dad always told us as kids, "Don't go down to anyone's level unless you're going down there to help bring them up." Dad's words still guide my interactions. As much as you can, shield yourself from traumatic events and stories, refer others to professional care, and take time to decompress after learning of traumatic experiences.

- *Find thought partners.* Sometimes, our Why needs more inspiration. Find colleagues who want to partner with you and collaborate on ways to support each other. Find those actively pursuing their Why, and you might be inspired with new reasons to look forward to school each day.

Spirituality as Part of Self-Care

My dad started a tiny one-room church in our front yard in 1963. It still stands today as a rock in our community in Jamaica. He strung up a big tarp attached to the side of our board house, and that space served as a church by night and a preschool by day. He hauled in cinder blocks and chopped thick planks of wood to make seats, and it was there that I learned to pray and rely on my faith.

As little preschoolers, we would kneel on the dirt floor and recite, "Our Father, thou art in Heaven, hallowed be thy name ... For thine is the Kingdom, and the power, and the glory, forever, amen."

At noon we would pray again, "For health and strength and daily food we praise thy name, O Lord, amen." (If you wanted to cause your teacher grief, you would interject with, "For health and strength and dollars and cents, we praise thy name, O Lord, amen," and all of your friends would burst out laughing, much to the chagrin of your teacher.)

After a full day of learning our ABCs, running and playing outside, and rolling around in the big, black tire dad used on his donkey cart, kids were ready to head home. We said our evening prayer, "Now the day is over, night is drawing nigh ... amen."

Kids pranced from under the tarp and headed home. Since it was my yard, I slipped through the front door to take off my uniform.

Connecting to and leaning on my faith not only followed the day, but it also followed me all the way throughout my formal education, into my college years, and now into my professional life. Prayer has kept me. It's a continuous process of prayer and faith to create the healing that my mind, soul, and body need to function. I'm a practicing Christian; I make no bones about my faith, and it's what has buffered me. It's this faith and a deep belief that prayer changes things that I taught my own children. Over the years, whether they were taking an exam, felt sad, or were conflicted about issues, they would ask me to pray for them, after which I'd anoint them with olive oil. Though church must legally be separated from school, I pray often and hope that my own students can connect to faith as a way of healing. I don't feel that everyone needs to be Christian. I just know that the power of prayer, of connecting to a higher power or something bigger and more powerful than we are, means you have something to lean on in troubled times.

In moments of hurt and pain, it's reassuring to know that you have someone or something that is mightier than you, someone or something that possesses supernatural powers to heal both your body and soul. My superpower is Jehovah, as is my steadfast belief that faith without work is dead and work without faith is dead. This faith has helped me in the most tumultuous periods of my life. As much as I have had issues with some level of attachment, I would be lost without the attachment that I have with my faith, my family, and my friends.

I'm not alone. Shannon was a soft-spoken, deliberate, and super organized teacher whom I was lucky to co-teach with when I started at Central. She knew everything about the school and was ready to share with me, the newbie. Shannon and I immediately struck up a solid friendship. Pretty soon she was my prayer partner, my prayer warrior. We were both Christian women who practiced our faith and leaned on it in moments of despair as well as moments of gratitude. We started a practice where we'd arrive at school earlier than usual once each week and head to the basement classroom that we shared for prayer time. We prayed for ourselves, we prayed for each other, and we prayed for our school and its administration. Through some of my toughest moments dealing with complex trauma of my own and from the students, those prayer sessions gave me the strength to continue.

Whatever you believe, I cannot recommend more highly that you lean on spirituality and allow yourself to experience the healing power of prayer. Even in the darkest moments, if you believe there is a higher power out there, you will find the strength to keep going. If you are able, find like-minded colleagues to support you in this practice as well.

Dealing with Loss in Schools: It's Okay to Mourn

While I argue that self-care can help support us as we engage in our heart work, none of us are immune to the loss of loved ones. In those moments of dire despair, when you feel like the rug has just been yanked from under your feet and there's a gaping hole engulfing you, remember that it's okay to mourn. It's difficult, but I've come to the realization that mourning is a part of the healing process. I've shared my painful path through grief and loss throughout this book, and it's something that I now openly share with the explicit hope that my story may invariably help others going through the same fate.

Writing about loss is difficult, especially tragic losses. However, writing this book has also been cathartic. Here, I'll share with you some of the profound losses that have not only impacted me but also given me reason and purpose.

Like my students, I've always lived in the urban core. Due to government neglect of the poor, it's almost impossible not to be in close proximity to community violence, often with deaths resulting. Writing this book has unearthed traumatic memories of loved ones lost tragically to the scourge of gun violence. It's my hope that this book—and this section in particular—provides some lessons and suggestions on how to grieve. It must be noted, however, that grieving is a deeply personal experience. There's no universal right or wrong way to grieve, and neither is there a fixed timeline when grieving starts or stops after losing loved ones. Each individual's journey through grief is uniquely shaped by waves of emotions, memories, and coping mechanisms. The only thing that we can do for each other is to be supportive.

I was fourteen when I lost my beloved granduncle to gun violence. I don't remember crying after that fateful morning. I simply turned to writing. Decades later and far away from my homeland, I began losing my students to gun violence. The first student I lost to gun violence was Tyson. I won't ever forget the emptiness I felt in my heart and my gut when I was told that he'd been shot and killed. He was a beautiful Black boy from Haiti. His smile lit up the classroom, and he was smart and full of promise. Then there was Eric. It took me a while to even pass the place where a pair of his sneakers hung as a makeshift memorial to honor his young life, gone way too soon. Eric, the tall, light-skinned Latine boy, a gentle giant who always asked, "Miss, do you have any Jolly Ranchers?" His favorite was apple flavor, which is mine too. Then there was Danny, who was tiny but had willpower, which, with the right set of opportunities, could have been a force for the common good.

I've lost so many of my students to gun violence over the years. I've lost good friends and colleagues, some tragically. Then, between 2020 and 2023, I lost my precious mom, auntie, and sister. In those moments of immense loss, I swore that the universe had turned on me. My emotional self was in a shambles. I tried hard every day to put on a brave face, but quietly I was falling apart.

The loss of loved ones is undeniably traumatic. Unresolved trauma eats at your very soul and has the power to cast people struggling with mental health issues into a perpetual state of emotional turmoil. Nonetheless, all is not lost, and in the midst of darkness and gloom, there exist glimmers of hope. Through the guidance and support of highly skilled, compassionate, and culturally responsive mental health counseling, individuals, including children who have experienced loss, can overcome the grip of trauma and propel themselves on the path to thriving.

I think that active listening and letting kids know that it's human to experience a wide array of emotions is very important. When appropriate, I let students know that, as their teacher, even I'm not immune to loss. Since the loss of my mom, aunt, and sister, I find myself carrying packets of tissues in my book bag in the same way I carry pens, pencils, and highlighters. These come in really handy as I console myself, grieving kids or even friends. Following up and checking in should be routine, but not in an overwhelming way. Having experienced so many personal losses, I've come to realize that having space to cry privately is as important without being overwhelmed by conversations about my losses. It's like threading needles, of course, but as educators, you know your students, and you will be able to know the times when checking in is okay, timely, and appropriate.

I've seen schools memorialize both teachers and students in ways that celebrate and honor their lives. In one school, I saw an entire wing of the school dedicated to the memory of a teacher who died. When my sister passed away, my school provided support for me, and the students did a fashion show in her memory. My family has provided financial support to a senior who survived a near-death experience to memorialize my sister's legacy of excellence and resilience.

I try as much as possible to normalize grief. I speak routinely about my loved ones, sharing pictures and stories on social media to keep their memories alive. In sharing, I'm also mindful of the fact that not all families share the same loving and positive relationships with their loved ones. In addition, death and traumatic loss can trigger trauma memories in others, so be sure to create a respectful and inclusive space where everyone's feelings and emotions are respected.

Truthfully, I think you live and learn to manage the pain of loss. I don't for one moment think anyone overcomes it. It's a constant battle, one that you learn to understand, live with, and make peace with in order to grow and thrive. But though loss stays with us, I also believe that anyone can move from trauma to healing, to living a life exemplified by grace, gratitude, and purpose. For me, pain and joy have to exist in the same place: in my heart.

What helps to emotionally support ourselves through trauma is perhaps different for everyone, but here are some ideas you may wish to try:

- *Lean on your community.* I've always had a community that supported me, both online and offline. Sharing my traumas in public provided me with the space where my community was able to not only support me but also to mourn with me.

- *Find solace in what lights you up.* I also turn to things I love to do in times of grief and pain, including writing, cooking, and dancing. Writing has been my path to healing ever since I lost my granduncle when I was fourteen.

- *Don't dwell on those things that you cannot control.* Rather, move strategically, deliberately, and intentionally to conquer fears and own space. It's not easy. It's a continuous work in progress. I'm constantly checking my mindset, removing self-doubts, and tuning into my purpose.

- *Honor those you've lost.* I find small ways to do this each day, such as wearing my mom's hats and clothes. This brings me a lot of comfort. You might also light candles for or write letters to your loved ones who have passed on. Cook their favorite meal and enjoy it while remembering them. Bring flowers to their resting place. Even just talking to them as though they are there can bring peace.

- *Give yourself grace.* Everyone reacts to trauma and grief differently, and there's no schedule for when you should feel and act "normal" again. Allow yourself to feel what you feel. Allow your body to rest.

If you feel that you've lost all sense of purpose when faced with trauma or the death of students or loved ones, don't hesitate to seek out professional mental health services. For my part, it hasn't been easy, but I'm gradually working through my pain while renewing my sense of purpose.

###

I hope that you've discovered some strategies that will help you in the challenges that are surely headed your way. I also hope that reading this book has allowed you to see that you aren't alone; teachers all over the United States and the world are also struggling and striving to provide a better path forward for their students and themselves. My true goal in writing these chapters is to help educators find a way toward their own resilience so they can heal, grow, thrive, and, in turn, help their students become happy, healthy, educated, and thriving adults.

Some Final Helpful Tips from Teachers

- *Wear clothes that lift your spirits,* and always choose comfortable shoes.

- *Begin each day with something that brings you joy.*

- *Bring your own lunch whenever possible,* as you don't have enough time for take-out.

- *Be willing to laugh at your own jokes*—even if no one else does!

- *Find time to dance*—with your students, with your loved ones, with yourself.

- *Buy yourself flowers.* If it makes you smile, it's worth it!

AFTERWORD

I'VE BEEN THROUGH a lot in my life. I've witnessed many horrible and traumatic events growing up in Jamaica. I saw the worst of humanity, but I also witnessed the best. I saw the way neighbors cared for each other and loved each other every single day. At birth, the cards were already stacked up against me, but my deep abiding faith in God and sheer determination not to become a statistic changed the trajectory of my life. I didn't succeed on my own. It took more than a village to raise me, and here I stand: a teacher, change-maker, trailblazer, and status quo disruptor!

Healing from trauma is a long, arduous journey with numerous twists and turns. It's not like a walk in the park on a beautiful summer day, nor is it chasing pretty painted butterflies. It's backbreaking, strenuous work. It's different for everyone, and we all must chart our individual paths to healing and peace. For some, it's years and years of mental health therapy and counseling, falling down and getting up, losing but winning. For me, healing is ongoing. I'm still on that journey, still a work in progress, but I'm thriving and in total control of my God-intended destiny.

I find solace, continued healing, and peace in writing and sharing my own story of survival and my continued fight against systemic racism, structural poverty, and gun violence. I continue to find healing in teaching kids.

I wish I had the luxury of being just a mom and now a grandmother. I don't. Like so many others, I'm juggling many balls, deciding which ones to hold up and which ones I will let fall in support of my mental health. This book chronicles elements of my journey as a public-school teacher, mother, grandmother, wife, justice seeker, and former lawmaker in Rhode Island. I'm sharing my own experiences growing up traumatized and living in poverty and with the constant "bussing" (firing) of gunshots in my neighborhood. Writing this book has been quite difficult, as trauma memories have resurfaced and I found there were times I had to step away. However, writing this book has also provided therapy and solace.

With the love and support of my family and the folks who want the best for me, I'm here and thriving. With their support, I know I can continue pushing against the winds of injustice, ripping up the narrative that was set for me at birth, and writing my own story. I don't take sharing my story and laying it bare for all the world to see lightly. It's my hope that within these pages lie hope, joy, resilience, and transformative power. I share my story with the world to let children know that with the right support and determination, they can move from post-traumatic stress to post-traumatic growth and healing. I share my story to let educators of all kinds know that we can create positive changes in our own lives and in the lives of others.

A trauma-informed school is not a tagline. It's a living, moving thing that has to be practiced, lived, and breathed by everyone in the school. It's the foundation on which schools should be built so that students are able to thrive. Within that context, kindness must be shown to everyone. We must lead with our hearts and be inclusive, for it's in that inclusivity that we are teaching our students not just how to survive but how to respond to each other in a positive way. This will create a better future for generations to come.

Educators, you know that challenges will always be a part of the job. Sometimes, it's trying to cut through red tape; sometimes, it's not having the right supplies; sometimes, it's encountering children who are struggling; sometimes, it's struggling through your own issues.

After all the personal experiences that I've had with trauma and with secondary trauma, I have come to learn that there can be healing from trauma. I'm a living witness that the journey of healing continues. People, including teachers, saw the best in me in spite of my limitations, in spite of the fact that I grew up poor, experienced poverty, and often went to bed with the sounds of gunshots echoing inside my community. Despite all that, I consider myself blessed. I also had caring adults in my life who saw beyond all the barriers in front of me and knew that I could overcome them. In the end, our collective liberation is what I'm working toward, and what I hope you, too, are working toward. I'm dedicated to cultivating a collective shift in perspective while encouraging all of us occupying spaces in schools to always use a trauma-informed lens.

I poured my heart and soul into this book because I think it will be a valuable resource to everyone, especially people involved in the care and education of our children. It's my hope that every single page will guide educators and other readers to a greater understanding of how trauma and stress impact children and their ability to concentrate and learn. More importantly, it is my hope that this book illustrates what we can all do collectively to effectively educate kids.

Transforming Schools: A Trauma-Informed Approach to

Teaching, Learning, and Healing will connect you, the reader, to the intersectionality of the social determinants of race, class, and economics within teaching and learning—and thereby, future outcomes for students. Understanding this intersectionality is especially important for teaching Black, brown, Indigenous, and foster children, as well as those receiving special education services. It's my hope that all teachers, particularly those without the shared or lived experiences of their students, acknowledge and change not only their perceptions of the children they teach but also their pedagogy.

If your school is not a trauma-informed school or your state doesn't have a Trauma-Informed Schools Act, that's okay. It's never too late. Ask yourself, *"Where can I start? What kind of practices can I put in place in my classroom? Who can I talk to about a broader program that would benefit kids across the whole school? Who will be my allies in this?"* Every movement starts with a single thought and a single person. We all have the chance to make a difference.

As a little girl growing up on the island, I was in close proximity to nature. I've watched in awe at the metamorphosis of caterpillars into beautiful multi-colored butterflies. Of course, schools differ vastly from butterflies, however a parallel is drawn to the necessity for a radical commitment to changing schools using trauma-informed approaches. This analogy serves as a reminder that, like the metamorphosis of caterpillars, transforming schools requires dedication, resilience, and an all-hands-and-hearts-on-deck approach.

To help transform schools and help rewrite the narrative is no small feat. Nonetheless, I wouldn't have dedicated time and effort in writing this book if I didn't believe in our collective ability to transform schools into nurturing spaces where children whose lives have been upended by trauma and toxic stress can heal, grow, learn, and thrive and where educators prioritize their own mental and physical health well-being. To every cherished educator reading this book, know that every word is written with love and a steadfast conviction that transforming schools is possible. I wholeheartedly encourage you to embrace the ideas and self-care principles in *Transforming Schools.*

I hope that this book inspires educators near and far to believe that the children they teach need—and deserve—infinite amounts of love and support to thrive. It's also my fervent hope that this book helps educators prioritize their own health and well-being, and that they understand they are not alone on this rewarding but challenging journey. Thank you, educators, for your willingness to learn, grow, and be that positive change for future generations. It's going to take a lot of work, but your drive, tenacity, and audacious spirit will guide you—and it will guide us all.

Let's embark on this transformative journey of healing, learning, growing, and thriving together. Years from now, I firmly believe that we will look back and witness the lives we've touched and the hopes we've rekindled in children, enabling them to live purposeful and meaningful lives.

FOOTPRINTS

I want to leave my footprints in the sand,
I want to hold you when you fall.
I want to be the shoulder you cry on,
And, yes, I want to be your friend.

I want to hold you in my arms,
Protect you from the storm.
I want to be everything you've ever dreamed of,
And, yes, I want to be your friend.

APPENDIX A

SURVEY QUESTIONS AND RESPONSES

THE FOLLOWING ARE the five survey questions that I asked each respondent to answer, along with a selection of their answers. If you haven't already, I recommend that you take fifteen minutes to journal about your answers to the survey questions below, too. This is something that you can revisit each year when you are beginning your planning for the new school year. See how your answers change over time to evaluate your progress.

1). Why did you decide to become a teacher?

2). Where did you first learn about trauma-informed learning, and was it in your teacher education program?

3). How do you respond to children in your school who have traumatic and/or adverse childhood experiences?

4). Do you think that you're adequately prepared to teach or interact with children experiencing trauma?

5). What is your idea of a trauma-informed school?

School Principal

1). I love seeing growth in people and teaching is one way to encourage and witness this growth. I enjoy seeing people's minds and understandings expand and being a part of the profession that does this excites me. I can recognize what *some* teachers did for me in my life to encourage my growth in these areas and I admired the work that they did.

2). I did not learn anything at all about trauma and children in my teacher education programs. I only learned about it when I was already a teacher and I engaged in some workshops. I was only one of two teachers from a very large staff that received this training and I recall thinking how much everybody should really be receiving it.

3). As a teacher, I would seek assistance from a counselor in order to make sure that the child has a trained professional to turn to and to discuss the traumatic experience and aftermath with. As a principal, I had two professionals in the area conduct professional learning for my entire staff in approaches to responding to students who have been impacted by trauma. We followed up with discussions within my staff and determined next steps for some of the students.

4). I am prepared to teach students who have had trauma, specifically via various modes of instruction and interaction within the classroom. By making time to first know my students so that they know that there is a caring atmosphere in my classroom, as well as opportunities for one-to-one work with them. These allow for the students to have chances to speak with me and to not have to be pressured to be "on the spot" when they're not ready to have the spotlight on them. These are just a couple of examples.

5). Being a trauma-informed school means that as an entire staff, we understand that our children bring with them the "unsettledness" that exists within their lives. Some stem from extreme crisis situations, while others may be more "quiet" and less notable. Regardless of the level, these experiences unsettle the minds and the spirits of our children, which often causes them to not be prepared to focus on academic content, engage in social interactions in a positive way (with peers or with staff members), or to feel comfortable within themselves.

Nonprofit Leader and Former Teacher

1). I taught for eight years before switching to the nonprofit side of education and decided to become a teacher in college at the suggestion of a professor who found I really loved helping peers improve their writing. I stayed teaching for those years because I love empowering students to take civic action in their communities and for themselves.

2). Trauma-informed was not part of my teaching preparatory program but seemed to gain a lot of importance in 2017. It was the focus of many professional developments, my school made it a school-wide initiative, and people were trying to give certificates for educators who had completed coursework in trauma-informed practices.

3). In the schools I taught at, the majority of students had been exposed to some level of trauma in their lives. It was imperative to lead with compassion, patience, and deescalation. Trauma can present as students being disengaged or disruptive, and in both cases it's important to try to figure out why and what's going on with them, and offer to listen, support, and work together to help them regulate themselves in a way that will allow them to access their education or connect them to available resources so that they can get the help they need because in 100 of 100 cases, students do not create these circumstances for themselves.

4). Now I do think I am adequately prepared, but you can always be learning more. Early on in my teaching I was not prepared, and did not understand how vast this problem is. The majority of students in classrooms have had at least one Adverse Childhood Experience, and most students have had a number of them. When you are early on in teaching, without that statistic and understanding, you create narratives that tell you students are intentionally checking out of their lessons. Dr. Ross Greene's "kids do well if they can" is an incredibly important concept to understand for educators.

5). A trauma-informed school to me is one where unpacking what is going on with a student is the norm, not the exception. Students are constantly kicked out of the room, suspended, given punishments for behaviors that relate back to traumatic experiences. In a trauma-informed school, the students, teachers, staff, administrators, counselors, and families would all work to be listening, practicing patience, and trying to find the why for behaviors that stem from trauma. It doesn't have to be a big thing; it just has to be a daily intention.

Education Major

1). My initial desire to become a teacher was inspired by the love of education and learning that my parents had instilled into me from a young age. As the son of two immigrants, I learned from a young age the value of education. Through my education, I would be able to achieve future success, but also, I would be able to accomplish all the dreams my parents had in this new land. My future would be the product of their struggles and hard work in starting a new life in a new land. My future was the center of their American Dream. My school district had a moderately diverse student body but had predominantly white faculty. In fact, I did not have a BIPOC teacher until college. As a result, there was often a disconnect between the faculty and the students they served. Although I was very fortunate to have supportive and understanding teachers, they oft had trouble understanding my unique struggles as a BIPOC student. This is when I began aspiring to be a teacher. I wanted BIPOC students to be able to see themselves in roles that they are historically underrepresented in. I wanted to be to my students what I never had in my education. What is the heart of education, if not to raise up a future generation of students to surpass the abilities of the generation that preceded them?

2). I was first introduced to student trauma in a freshman survey course, mandatory for all Education majors, titled Educational Psychology. In this course, we were introduced to the various psychological principles at play in education. However, I did not actively engage into trauma-informed practices until I enrolled in an elective course titled Urban Education. In this course, we spent considerable time engaging in the best trauma-informed practices in Urban Educational settings. Moreover, we took considerable time analyzing the unique traumas faced by specific racial, ethnic, and socio-economic groups.

3). I think the most important thing we can do for our students, especially those who have gone through traumatic and adverse experiences is being present. Students in this position often need someone they can trust and find support in. If we are not present for our students, how can we expect them to trust us or come to us for support? Once this relationship has formed, then we must do everything in our power to ensure our students' success. As educators, it is our responsibility to accommodate all students. We often think about this in terms of our content areas and find different pedagogical approaches to translate our content knowledge to students who have not interacted with the material before. How often, however, do we also consider our students' well-being within this framework? If a student's trauma or experiences prevents them from engaging a specific concept or lesson, then it is our responsibility as educators to find different means of engagement.

4). Although I have undergone significant preparations to interact with children experiencing trauma, truthfully, I still feel inadequately prepared. Students are constantly going through a changing social-emotional landscape that is gradually becoming more and more different than the landscape I had gone through as a student. As a result, the techniques and strategies I have been taught may not be effective or applicable in the future. For this reason, I feel inadequacy, as it constantly pressures me as a teacher to continue to learn and grow to provide the best evidence-based practices in my classroom. Realistically, it is impossible to guarantee that every student is able to get the help and support they need, but it is possible to guarantee that every student at least has the opportunity. Therefore, as educators, we constantly have to be in a state of growth and learning to truly be prepared to engage students who have experienced and are experiencing trauma.

5). My idea of a trauma-informed school is an institution that is committed to ensuring the success of all students within a classroom. This means providing equitable and differentiated means of approaching students in regard to both content knowledge and well-being. It is clear that the epidemic of trauma among students does not have a clear one-stop solution, therefore we need to start considering this issue as a process rather than a box to check off. We must continually grow our skill set and adapt our responses as an educational institution to accommodate the ever-changing needs of our students and community. We must continue to research and apply the best evidence-based practices within our classrooms and school systems. Moreover, we must be willing to learn, recognize our downfalls, and make tangible, demonstrable changes to remove the systemic barriers that prevent students from seeking help and support. Above all, we must ensure that every student has the opportunity to succeed regardless of their backgrounds, experiences, and traumas. This is the heart of teaching.

Elementary School Teacher

1). As a child growing up and attending school, I admired my teachers. Their deportment, characters and how they try to put the lessons across so that we can understand them. Their relationship with us were exceptional. To add to those, two of my older sisters were teachers to whom I looked up to. I am teaching for 36 years up to present. Children are fun and adorable. After I started my teaching career in a normal school setting, I found it important to obtain more knowledge because of what I have observed. I then expounded my knowledge in Special Education program. Thus, I realized that trauma/trauma-informed affect some students. Teaching and observing child/children help me to recognize a child/children who are: confused, have difficulty concentrating, with anxiety or fear, those withdrawn from other students, and those who are sad at all times.

2). Understanding what some children have seen going on in their environment, and the adverse experiences due to external forces most of the time result in total or partial disability. Thus, this can negatively affect their educational performance. To help these children with these psycho-social difficulties such as witnessing a terrible event, rape, or even a fall from a staircase, it is important that you as the teacher finds a way to allow your students to trust you.

3). A program can also be set up with other personnel to help students overcome their traumatic experiences. Let's think of a child falling from a staircase and is very traumatized when seeing a staircase. You can safely say to the child, "It is okay to fall, but next time when you are coming down a staircase, remember to hold on to the rails and you will be safe."

4). Once you understand the challenges and difficulties of these students it is easier to work with them. I find it necessary to use different strategies to control their behavior, [such as]: use effective intervention, use visual learning support, allow them to participate in social interaction. Identifying and serving students with traumatic behavioral problems will make the school environment safer.

5). Trauma-informed schools consider what students and staff might be facing in their lives. These schools are the ones in which all parties involved recognize and respond to the impact of traumatic stress on those who have contact with the system. It is also a place where all students feel safe, welcomed, and supportive. Ongoing inquiry is a must in this school environment, which should lead to teamwork, coordination, creativity, and where sharing must take place. Continuous learning for educators and students should be a must.

Also, it is important to engage parents as partners, because one parent experience does not have to be the same as the other. It is also important to navigate social settings in order to find out what some parents are dealing with outside of the school. Having dialogue with parents on children's behavior pattern will lead up to improvement at home and school. Remember parents know everything in the child's spectrum, so it is important for them to spend time understanding their children.

History Teacher

1). I decided to become a teacher because I have a love for history and older children. I wanted to share (in a "fun" way) that history can be interesting. I was a substitute for thirteen years and have taught at Windsor for three years.

2). I first learned about trauma and the effects from trauma in my many psychology classes. It must have been mentioned in my education classes at some point, but I don't exactly remember (it's been a while—class of 2002).

3). I respond to student's trauma in many ways. I try to build a relationship with the student first. If they want to talk about it, I listen. Sometimes I share my experiences. I always meet them where they are at and treat them as an equal human.

4). I do believe I am adequately prepared to teach and interact with children experiencing trauma. Going through Windsor myself as a teenager, plus my education, training and experience as a mother of five, I am not usually surprised by anything and can be empathetic. I am real at all times, but try to see the positive in any situation.

5). Windsor is a great example of a trauma-informed school. We have yearly trainings, we do our research on a child's situation, and we meet to discuss strategies on how we can best help the student to be successful.

High School Director of Education

1). I have wanted to be a teacher since I was a child. I would play school for hours. I have been working in the education field for twenty years. I started in a public-school setting and transitioned to a special education day school after being laid off. When the opportunity came to get hired back, I declined the offer because I enjoyed working with the kids at Sutherland and I loved the school and community at Sutherland. I taught at the school for approximately 8 years before transitioning to more administrative roles.

2). I first learned about trauma at Sutherland. It was not in my teacher education program.

3). I respond to kids in my school who have traumatic and/or adverse experiences first by speaking to them in a calm manner. I take time to develop a relationship with the student so that they can start trusting me. Also, I like to focus on student strengths and having a positive attitude.

4). I feel that I am adequately prepared to teach and interact with children experiencing trauma.

5). Sutherland has had trauma-informed be the focus of our school for years and we have done many trainings on how to be trauma-informed.

Special Education Middle School English Teacher

1). I became a teacher because I've always liked to teach and help others. As a middle school and high school student, I completed a lot of community services helping teachers as a TA at the nearby elementary school. I enjoyed it. Growing up in San Diego, I also noticed that none of my teachers were Mexican, so I decided that I would pursue teaching to change that as well. I am now on my fifteenth year of teaching.

2). Trauma-informed teaching was not in my teacher education program. I have had one PD session (this year) on trauma-informed teaching—it was great, but nothing before that.

3). Many of our students are dealing with trauma—same as I did growing up in a dysfunctional home with home and food insecurity. I try to be very tactful and understanding of everyone's situation. I've been there.

4). Honestly, I don't think that I am adequately prepared to counsel children regarding their trauma. Although I personally experienced trauma growing up, I know that not everyone responds to trauma the same way.

Math Teacher

1). I decided to become a teacher because I enjoyed working with children and wanted to make sure that students didn't struggle with math like I did in school. I became math chairperson/Lead teacher because I had tremendous experience and success in teaching math to students in every category of need.

2). I did not learn about trauma in my teacher education program. I learned about trauma as part of my staff development training while on the job.

3). It depends on the situation. In some cases, we are not allowed to bring it up or address it if it does not relate specifically to the students in my charge. In other cases, we are required to let the counselor handle it.

4). I don't believe that I am adequately prepared. Learning about it and being in the situation are two totally different experiences. However, if the situation requires my intervention, then my only choice will be to follow protocol according to the training I received.

5). My idea is one in which the students and teachers know the protocols and know what procedures to take depending on the type of trauma.

Early Childhood Teacher's Assistant

1). I have been a teacher assistant in the early childhood field for about thirty years. I am currently in a training program to get my teaching degree

2). I learned about trauma especially in children rather young because my mother was a foster parent, so I got to see what that looked like very young. I mostly saw it in young children, which is why I chose this field.

3). There is no real program that deals with trauma but we have a program that address behaviors and most of the children we see with behaviors have experienced some trauma. We have begun using mindfulness in classrooms, as well as conscious discipline. I feel it works for some children but we need to do more.

4). I can speak for most of my coworkers and say No we do not have the skills or enough knowledge and training to deal with this issue. We do have clinicians but they are not in the classrooms enough

5). We could be considered informed but there is plenty of room for improvement. Sometimes things come out in the Children's play and the response time to help them is way too late because of paperwork and protocols. Some children are dealing with trauma for way too long with no intervention because parents are unaware that the child was affected. Because it is said that children under five are not aware of things that happen around them. It is not addressed until they exhibit behaviors. What would happen if we address it before the behaviors manifest and let them know we see them and we care!

High School English Teacher

1). Cliche; since third grade. But sitting in my high school, I said to the class that "I would come back to teach in this school."

2). Trauma discussions became part of my awareness in 2008, working in Massachusetts and it was a series of PDs.

3). I do listen best I can. But knowing intimate details of someone in pain, I have to forward to the school's psychiatrist or social worker. I call the nurse to communicate my understanding, write it down. It's nerve wracking—happened twice in which I then was part of a conversation w/mothers who came in. Meanwhile and during the meetings I greet warmly, offer and accept hugs.

4). Am I adequately prepared to teach someone experience traumatic stress? No.

5). Definitely there had to be a conversation about how to navigate presenting to individuals—each need will differ. I feel like I'm on eggshells when I'm aware of a student's pain. I need more tools than just a notice that the student is in a delicate state.

High School English Teacher

1). I decided to become a teacher because I wanted to help students become literate and educated community members—ones who could critically approach the world and advocate for themselves and others.

2). I first learned about the term "trauma-informed" three or four years ago in my school when colleagues began an initiative to increase awareness of the effects of student trauma. My teacher education program did not include a specific course or unit in trauma-informed education.

3). When I am teaching content that maybe triggering, I usually do the following:

- Provide "trigger warnings" before reading/discussing adverse experiences.

- Allow alternate assignments/alternate spaces for students who are uncomfortable with class topics.

- Refer students to support staff and school psychologists when they are in need of safe spaces.

- De-escalate a student's reactionary responses to class/assignment stresses.

4). A good deal of work has been done in my school to help teachers learn to address student needs. I believe my practice is a work in progress and that I have more to learn.

5). One in which all stakeholders are aware of and react to ALL barriers to learning (academic, social, and emotional) so that students can maximize their educational potential.

Retired Sign Language Teacher

1). I decided to become a teacher of the deaf for several reasons. I had studied anthropology and linguistics as an undergraduate, and done independent research on cross-cultural communication in school settings as a graduate student in applied anthropology. I was interested in sign language, and also wanted to work with children. These interests converged in becoming a teacher of the deaf. I taught for two years in the Parent Guidance program for families whose little ones had been recently diagnosed with an educationally significant hearing loss. I then worked as a sign language interpreter at the community college level for 8 years. I went back to teaching at a school for the deaf children, teaching at the middle school and high school levels for 26 years.

2). In my teacher-education program I did not learn about trauma/trauma-informed education. My masters degree training was in the early to mid-1970's. We were well taught that deaf and hard of hearing students needed to be evaluated by an educational psychologist who thoroughly understood the complexities of assessing children with pre-lingually acquired hearing loss. Factors within the family as well as within the child needed to be taken into account.

3). A number of children at the school for the deaf came with significant emotional trauma from their family situations. This was in addition to the emotional difficulties that most hearing parents have when needing to make adjustments to family life when learning their child has an educationally significant hearing loss. There will need to be adjustments in communication, which affects all aspects of family life. Some families were more able to make these adjustments than others. Fortunately, even though the school had a small total enrollment (under 100) from preschool through high school, there was a full complement of professional staff who could work with children as needed: psychologist, social worker, linguist, guidance counselor, and behavior therapists. Teachers could call on these professionals when they noticed issues with the students in their class. (Class size was typically 5–7.)

4). I did not have any training that prepared me to work with children experiencing trauma. Neither did I have training regarding confidentiality of records. I think this could be an issue with trauma-informed teaching if data is collected and stored digitally.

5). A trauma-informed school is one that takes the social/emotional well-being of all students seriously. Teachers would notice behavior that indicates the child is having emotional difficulties, and there would be a recognized policy for referral to the appropriate professional for evaluation and follow-up. There should be no stigma attached to this. As I mentioned in answering question number 4, great care would need to be taken to ensure that information on the child would only be shared with those within the school with a need to know.

Liberal Arts Teacher

1). I chose to become a teacher because I love to make a difference in the world. I also want to teach my students that self-love is important because I grew up hating myself because I wished I was white.

2). Learned about it from you, Marcia!

3). I listen and refer them to school social worker or guidance.

4). I think I am because I've also experienced trauma in my life, but I'm excited to learn more about it so I can help my students even more.

5). I think it's a great idea and I look forward to learning more.

Suburban Elementary School Teacher

1). I decided to become a teacher because I love little children. Their innocence, curiosity, and trust give me great joy.

2). I first learned about trauma in one of my teacher education courses through Zaretta Hammond's book "Culturally Responsive Teaching and the Brain."

3). I don't know if I am adequately prepared to teach children experiencing trauma, but I have had a few students who clearly were experiencing trauma.

4). My number one tool to deal with students experiencing trauma has always been to build relationships. I believe strongly in the strategy of checking in personally every morning with my students, and spending 5 minutes at the beginning of the day on a genuine conversation with them. Other strategies include modeling healthy recognition of my own adverse reactions to stress, and creating a physical calming space for students to take a few minutes to regulate themselves.

5). A trauma-informed school would lay heavy emphasis on building trusting relationships between staff and students and also provide teachers with plenty of resources, professional training, and administrative support when dealing with children who are experiencing trauma. All three things—resources, training and support—are critical. An intensive schoolwide program such as RULER would also give everyone—administrators, teachers and students—the tools to recognize, acknowledge, and regulate their emotions in healthy ways.

Substitute Special Education High School Teacher

1). I started substitute teaching in October of last year. I had no experience but I love it and have decided to stay.

2). During a special education meeting we discussed trauma among our students and a survey that ranks trauma. I took the survey while we were at a Professional Development day and the school psychologists discussed taking on students trauma and how we take that on as well.

3). I have a caseload of thirteen children as well as all the other students in the classes I support. I have tried to build relationships with all thirteen as well as anyone else who will let me in. I start with the basics of bringing snacks, water, and chrome books in order to get them ready to learn. I also spend one on one time to get to know them and hear what their needs are.

4). My degree is in psychology so I have some understanding of trauma but I agree there needs to be a lot more training in the schools. I also spent time as a youth and families minister and did a lot of training for that which I feel helped prepare me.

5). If we don't address our own trauma, we cannot help those around us. There needs to be more focus on this during trainings in order to best serve our students. We need to create safe places physically, mentally, and emotionally within the school for healing and growth. We need to provide clear structure and expectations for students to thrive while also acknowledging trauma in their lives.

APPENDIX B

THE ADVERSE CHILDHOOD EXPERIENCE (ACE) QUESTIONNAIRE

This questionnaire was developed as part of the original CDC-Kaiser ACE Study. It can be helpful in determining whether you or your students have undergone adverse childhood experiences.

It's important to note that discrimination, poverty, racism, or other systemic abuses can have similar outcomes to ACEs.

Give yourself one point for each "yes" answer.

The ACE Questionnaire

1). Did a parent or other adult in the household often or very often ... a) Swear at you, insult you, put you down, or humiliate you? or b) Act in a way that made you afraid that you might be physically hurt?

2). Did a parent or other adult in the household often or very often ... a) Push, grab, slap, or throw something at you? or b) Ever hit you so hard that you had marks or were injured?

3). Did an adult or person at least five years older than you ever ... a) Touch or fondle you or have you touch their body in a sexual way? or b) Attempt or actually have oral, anal, or vaginal intercourse with you?

4). Did you often or very often feel that ... a) No one in your family loved you or thought you were important or special? or b) Your family didn't look out for each other, feel close to each other, or support each other?

5). Did you often or very often feel that ... a) You didn't have enough to eat, had to wear dirty clothes, and had no one to protect you? or b) Your parents were too drunk or high to take care of you or take you to the doctor if you needed it?

6). Were your parents ever separated or divorced?

7). Was your parent/caregiver: a) Often or very often pushed, grabbed, slapped or had something thrown at him/her? or b) Sometimes, often, or very often kicked, bitten, hit with a fist, or hit with something hard? or c) Ever repeatedly hit over at least a few minutes or threatened with a gun or knife?

8). Did you live with anyone who was a problem drinker or alcoholic, or who used street drugs?

9). Was a household member depressed or mentally ill, or did a household member attempt suicide?

10). Did a household member go to prison?

RESOURCES

Dial 988 to reach the Suicide and
Crisis Lifeline immediately

Veterans Crisis Line: (800) 273-8255

Disaster Distress Helpline: (8000 985-5990

SAMHSA Helpline: (800) 662-4357

Trauma Institute: (413) 774-2340

SUGGESTED READING

Books

- Greenwald, Ricky. *Child Trauma Handbook: A Guide for Helping Trauma-Exposed Children and Adolescents.* Routledge, London, 2005

- Greenwald, Ricky. *Treating Problem Behaviors: A Trauma Informed Approach.* Routledge, London, 2005

- Jones, Ron. *The Acorn People.* Random House, New York, 1996

- Kendi, Ibram X. *How to Be an Antiracist.* One World, London, 2019

- Kendi, Ibram X. *Stamped From the Beginning: The Definitive History of Racist Ideas in America.* Hachette, New York, 2017

- McClintock, Karen A., *Trauma-Informed Pastoral Care: How to Respond When Things Fall Apart.* Fortress Press, Minneapolis, 2019

- Rothstein, Richard. *The Color of Law: A Forgotten History of How Our Government Segregated America.* Liveright/Norton, New York, 2018

- Van Der Kolk, Bessel. *The Body Keeps the Score: Brain, Mind, and Body in the Healing of Trauma.* Penguin Books, New York, 2015
- Wilkerson, Isabel. *Caste: The Origins of Our Discontents.* Random House, New York, 2020

For Kids

- Alifirenka, Caitlin and Ganda, Martin. *I Will Always Write Back.* Little Brown, New York, 2016
- Cherry-Paul, Sonja, Reynolds, Jason, and Kendi, Ibram X. *Stamped (For Kids!): Racism, Antiracism, and You.* Little Brown, New York, 2021
- Greenwald, Ricky, and Jones Baden, Katrina. *A Fairy Tale.* Trauma Institute and Children's Trauma Institute. ticti.org/resources/books/fairy-tale.
- Ranglin-Vassell, Marcia. *Journeys: A Collection of Poems about Life, Love, Faith and Determination*
- Stevenson, Bryan. *Just Mercy: A Story of Justice and Redemption.* One World, London, 2015

Online

- *Helping Traumatized Children Learn: A Report and Policy Agenda.* Massachusetts Advocates for Children: Trauma and Learning Policy Initiative in collaboration with Harvard Law School and The Task Force on Children Affected by Domestic Violence. traumasensitiveschools.org/wp-content/uploads/2013/06/Helping-Traumatized-Children-Learn.pdf.

- *Helping Traumatized Children Learn 2: Creating and Advocating for Trauma-Sensitive Schools.* Trauma and Learning Policy Initiative: a partnership of Massachusetts Advocates for Children and Harvard Law School. traumasensitiveschools.org/wp-content/uploads/2013/11/HTCL-Vol-2-Creating-and-Advocating-for-TSS.pdf

- "Secondary Traumatic Stress: A Fact Sheet for Child Serving Professionals." The National Child Traumatic Stress Network. nctsn.org/sites/default/files/resources/fact-sheet/secondary_traumatic_stress_child_serving_professionals.pdf.

SOURCES

- Administration for Children and Families. "Secondary Traumatic Stress." acf.hhs.gov/trauma-toolkit/secondary-traumatic-stress. Accessed November 15, 2023.

- American University. "Why is School Attendance Important? The Effects of Chronic Absenteeism. January 14, 2021. soeonline.american.edu/blog/importance-of-school-attendance/. Accessed November 15, 2023.

- Anderson, Patrick. "Rep Marcia Ranglin-Vassell, who Pulled off Historic Win in 2016, Not Seeking Reelection." June 16, 2022. providencejournal.com/story/news/politics/2022/06/15/providence-state-rep-marcia-ranglin-vassell-not-seeking-reelection/7637142001/. Accessed January 13, 2024

- APA. "For Black students, unfairly harsh discipline can lead to lower grades." October 7, 2021. apa.org/news/press/releases/2021/10/black-students-harsh-discipline#:~:text=WASHINGTON%20%E2%80%94%20Black%20students%20are%20often,by%20the%20American%20Psychological%20Association. Accessed November 15, 2023.

- Asmelash, Leah. "Indiana's 'red flag' law should have prevented the FedEx shooting. Here's what else you should know about these laws." CNN. April 21, 2021. cnn.com/2021/04/21/us/red-flag-laws-explainer-trnd/index.html. Accessed November 15, 2023.

- Bauer, Nerissa. "Childhood Adversity: Buffering Stress & Building Resilience" Healthy Children. July 26, 2021. healthychildren.org/English/healthy-living/emotional-wellness/Building-Resilience/Pages/ACEs-Adverse-Childhood-Experiences.aspx. Accessed November 15, 2023.

- Burns, Kalee, Liana Fox, and Danielle Wilson. "Expansions to Child Tax Credit Contributed to 46% Decline in Child Poverty Since 2020." September 13, 2022. census.gov/library/stories/2022/09/record-drop-in-child-poverty.html. Accessed November 15, 2023.

- Carini, Frank. "Environmental Racism Puts South Side's Health at Risk." Eco RI News. February 9, 2018. ecori.org/2018-2-8-environmental-racism-live-and-well-on-the-south-side. Accessed November 15, 2023.

- Carr, Sarah. "Public Schools Are Struggling to Retain Black Teachers. These Ex-Teachers Explain Why." *Time*. January 5, 2022. time.com/6130991/black-teachers-resigning. Accessed November 15, 2023.

- CASEL. "The Fundamentals of SEL." casel.org/fundamentals-of-sel. Accessed November 16, 2023.

- CDC. "Fast Facts: Preventing Adverse Childhood Experiences." June 29, 2023. cdc.gov/violenceprevention/aces/fastfact.html. Accessed November 15, 2023.

- CDC. The US Public Health Service Untreated Syphilis Study at Tuskegee Timeline. cdc.gov/tuskegee/timeline.htm#Overview. Accessed November 15, 2023.

- Children's Defense Fund. "The State of America's Children 2021." childrensdefense.org/state-of-americas-children-2021/soac-2021-child-poverty. Accessed November 15, 2023.

- Dixon, Elizabeth. "Breaking the Chains of Generational Trauma." *Psychology Today*. July 3, 2021. psychologytoday.com/us/blog/the-flourishing-family/202107/breaking-the-chains-generational-trauma. Accessed November 19, 2023.

- Faulkner, Tim. "Rhode Island Ranked in Top 10 for Asthma Rate." Eco RI News. February 15, 2019. ecori.org/2019-2-14-rhode-island-ranks-9th-for-asthma-cities-suffer-most. Accessed November 15, 2023.

- Ferris, Susan, Mitchell Corey, Yerardi, Joe. "When Schools Call Police on Kids. The Center for Public Integrity. September 8, 2021. publicintegrity.org/education/criminalizing-kids/police-in-schools-disparities/. Accessed January 14, 2024.

- Feeding America. "Hunger in America." feedingamerica.org/hunger-in-america. Accessed November 19, 2023.

- Flint Water Crisis: Everything You Need to Know. Nrdc.org/stories/flint-water-crisis-everything-you-need-know. Accessed November 19, 2023.

- Garrido, Sandra, Felicity A. Baker, Jane W. Davidson, Grace Moore, and Steve Wasserman. "Music and trauma: the relationship between music, personality, and coping style." *Frontiers in Psychology.* July 10, 2015. doi:10.3389/fpsyg.2015.00977.

- Gomez, Wendy. "Abolishing School Resource Officers Amidst the Black Lives Matter Movement: A History and Case Study in Oakland and Los Angeles." *Princeton University Journal of Public & International Affairs.* May 5, 2021. jpia.princeton.edu/news/abolishing-school-resource-officers-amidst-black-lives-matter-movement-history-and-case-study. Accessed November 19, 2023.

- Gordon, Joshua. "Addressing the Crisis of Black Youth Suicide." National Institute of Mental Health. September 22, 2020. nimh.nih.gov/about/director/messages/2020/addressing-the-crisis-of-black-youth-suicide. Accessed November 19, 2023.

- Healthy Children. "Constantly Connected: How Media Use Can Affect Your Child." May 30, 2023. healthychildren.org/English/family-life/Media/Pages/adverse-effects-of-television-commercials.aspx. Accessed November 19, 2023.

- Isobel, Sophie, Andrea McCloughen, Melinda Goodyear, and Kim Foster. "Intergenerational Trauma and Its Relationship to Mental Health Care: A Qualitative Inquiry." *Community Mental Health Journal.* May 2021. pubmed.ncbi.nlm.nih.gov/32804293. Accessed November 19, 2023.

- Jackson, Candace. "What Is Redlining?" *The New York Times.* August 17, 2021. nytimes.com/2021/08/17/realestate/what-is-redlining.html.

- LeBlanc, Atticus. "How Systemic Racism Exists in U.S. Housing Policies." *Forbes.* July 9, 2020. forbes.com/sites/forbesrealestatecouncil/2020/07/09/how-systemic-racism-exists-in-us-housing-policies/?sh=67247b556959.

- Leeb, Rebecca T., Rebecca H. Bitsko, Lakshmi Radhakrishnan, Pedro Martinez, Rashid Njai, and Kristin M. Holland. "Mental Health–Related Emergency Department Visits Among Children Aged <18 Years During the COVID-19 Pandemic—United States, January 1–October 17, 2020." CDC. cdc.gov/mmwr/volumes/69/wr/mm6945a3.htm. Accessed November 19, 2023.

- Lloyd, Chrishana, Marta Alvira-Hammond, Julianna Carson, and Deja Logan. "Family, Economic, and Geographic Characteristics of Black Families with Children." Child Trends. March 5, 2021. childtrends.org/publications/family-economic-and-geographic-characteristics-of-black-families-with-children. Accessed November 19, 2023.

- Luscombe, Belinda. "What's the Spike in Child Poverty in the U.S." September 12, 2023, time.com/6313242/child-poverty-rate-2022-census/. Accessed November 19, 2023.

- Machado, Steph. "Half of Providence Students Were Chronically Absent Last School Year." *Boston Globe.* September 20, 2023. bostonglobe.com/2023/09/20/metro/half-of-providence-students-were-chronically-absent-last-school-year. Accessed November 19, 2023.

- Massachusetts Advocates for Children. *Helping Traumatized Children Learn: A Report and Policy Agenda.* 2005. traumasensitiveschools.org/wp-content/uploads/2013/06/Helping-Traumatized-Children-Learn.pdf. Accessed November 19, 2023.

- Najarro, Ileana. "Here's How Many Hours a Week Teachers Work." Education Week. April 14, 2022. edweek.org/teaching-learning/heres-how-many-hours-a-week-teachers-work/2022/04. Accessed November 19, 2023.

- Najarro, Ileana and Hyon-Young Kim. "What a Typical Teacher's Day Actually Looks Like." EducationWeek. April 14, 2022. edweek.org/teaching-learning/what-a-typical-teachers-day-actually-looks-like/2022/04. Accessed November 19, 2023.

- National Archives. Civil Rights Act (1964). archives.gov/milestone-documents/civil-rights-act. Accessed November 19, 2023.

- Pignataro, Juliana Rose. "Providence School Shooting: Student Shot, Killed Outside School. newsweek.com/providence-school-shooting-student-shot-killed-outside-high-school-1108225. Accessed January 14, 2024.

- Thomas, Deja and Fry, Richard. "Prior to COVID-19, Child Poverty Rates Had Reached Record Low in US." pewresearch.org/short-reads/2020/11/30/prior-to-covid-19-child-poverty-rates-had-reached-record-lows-in-u-s/. Accessed January 14, 2024.

- National Conference of State Legislatures. "Youth Homelessness Overview." March 29, 2023. ncsl.org/human-services/youth-homelessness-overview. Accessed November 19, 2023.

- National Education Association. "Making Schools Safe and Just: Policing in Schools can Harm Children of Color- and Aspiring Educators are demanding Change." nea.org/nea-today/all-news-articles/making-schools-safe-and-just. Accessed November 19, 2023.

- National Geographic. "How the Pandemic Isolation is Affecting Young Kids Developing Minds." Nationgeographic. com/science/article/how-pandemic-isolation-is-affecting-young-kids-developing-minds. Accessed January 14, 2024.

- National Institute of Mental Health. "I'm So Stressed Out! Fact Sheet." Accessed November 11, 2023. nimh.nih.gov/health/ publications/so-stressed-out-fact-sheet#: ~:text=Stress%20 is%20the%20physical%20or,repeatedly%20over%20a%20 long%20time. Accessed January 14, 2024.

- National Network for Youth. "What Is Trauma? Stress Vs. Trauma." nn4youth.org/learn/trauma-informed-care-toolkit/ stress-vs-trauma. Accessed November 13, 2023.

- News in Health. "Teen Suicide: Understanding the Risk and Getting Help." The National Institute of Health. September 2019. newsinhealth.nih.gov/2019/09/teen-suicide. Accessed November 13, 2023.

- NPR. "The Price Of Poverty: What It Means To Be Poor In America." October 17, 2022. npr.org/2022/10/17/1129563570/ the-price-of-poverty-what-it-means-to-be-poor-in-america. Accessed November 13, 2023.

- Pinetree Institute. "ACEs and Trauma: The ACE Study." pinetreeinstitute.org/aces. Accessed November 15, 2023.

- Providence Public Schools. "Who We Are." providenceschools. org/domain/49. Accessed November 9, 2023.

- Rahman, Khaleda. "COVID Orphans—Over 200,000 U.S. Children Have Lost A Parent or Caregiver to the Pandemic." *Newsweek.* February 4, 2022. newsweek.com/covid-orphans-over-200000-children-lost-parent-caregiver-1675856. Accessed November 9, 2023.

- Reiss, Franziska, Ann-Katrin Meyrose, Christiane Otto, Thomas Lampert, Fionna Klasen, and Ulrike Ravens-Sieberer. "Socioeconomic status, stressful life situations and mental health problems in children and adolescents: Results of the German BELLA cohort-study." *PLOS One.* March 13, 2019. doi.org/10.1371/journal.pone.0213700. Accessed November 9, 2023.

- Rhode Island Kids Count. "Children's Mental Health in Rhode Island." October 2022. rikidscount.org/Portals/0/Uploads/Documents/Issue%20Briefs/11.22%20Mental%20Health%20Brief%20FINAL.pdf?ver=2022-11-15-121931-453. Accessed November 9, 2023.

- SAMHSA. "Recognizing and Treating Child Traumatic Stress." October 23, 2023. samhsa.gov/child-trauma/recognizing-and-treating-child-traumatic-stress. Accessed November 9, 2023.

- SAMHSA. "Trauma and Violence." September 22, 2022. samhsa.gov/trauma-violence. Accessed November 9, 2023.

- Save the Children. "Child Poverty in America." savethechildren.org/us/charity-stories/poverty-in-america. Accessed November 19, 2023.

- State of Rhode Island General Assembly. "Trauma Informed Schools Act signed into law." July 5, 2022. rilegislature.gov/pressrelease/_layouts/RIL.PressRelease.ListStructure/Forms/DisplayForm.aspx?List=c8baae31-3c10-431c-8dcd-9dbbe21ce3e9&ID=372951&Web=2bab1515-0dcc-4176-a2f8-8d4beebdf488#:~:. Accessed November 19, 2023.

- Tatter, Grace. "Low Income Students and a Special Education Mismatch." Harvard Graduate School of Education. February 21, 2019. gse.harvard.edu/ideas/usable-knowledge/19/02/low-income-students-and-special-education-mismatch. Accessed November 19, 2023.

- The National Child Traumatic Stress Network. "Secondary Traumatic Stress: A Fact Sheet for Child-Serving Professionals. nctsn.org/resources/secondary-traumatic-stress-fact-sheet-child-serving-professionals. Accessed January 14, 2024

- Title 16 Education. Health and Safety of Pupils. rilin.state.ri.us/Statutes/TITLE16/16-21/16-21-41.htm. Accessed January 14, 2024.

- UNICEF. "How the COVID-19 pandemic has scarred the world's children." March 10, 2021. unicef.org/coronavirus/COVID-19-pandemic-scarred-world-children. Accessed January 14, 2024.

- Urban Institute. "School Funding: Do Poor Kids Get Their Fair Share?" May 2017. apps.urban.org/features/school-funding-do-poor-kids-get-fair-share. Accessed January 14, 2024.

- US Census. "Mothers Maintain 80% of Single-Parent Family Groups." Census.gov/newsroom/press-releases/2022/americas-families-and-living-arrangements.html. Accessed January 14, 2024.

- U.S. Department of Health and Human Services. *Listen Up!: Youth Listening Session Toolkit.* Office of Population Affairs. September 2020. opa.hhs.gov/adolescent-health/positive-youth-development/meaningful-youth-engagement. Accessed January 14, 2024.

- U.S. Department of Housing and Urban Development. "History of Fair Housing." hud.gov/program_offices/fair_housing_equal_opp/aboutfheo/history. Accessed November 19, 2023.

- U.S. Surgeon General. "Social Media and Youth Mental Health." hhs.gov/surgeongeneral/priorities/youth-mental-health/social-media/index.html. Accessed November 13, 2023.

- Weiler, Spencer C., and M. Cray. "Police at School: A Brief History and Current Status of School Resource Officers." Semantic Scholar. May 2011. semanticscholar.org/paper/Police-at-School%3A-A-Brief-History-and-Current-of-Weiler-Cray/27d86306a3c0d37c5d89ad64a295549ff2f2a049. Accessed November 13, 2023.

- Youth.gov. "Children of Incarcerated Parents." youth.gov/youth-topics/children-of-incarcerated-parents. Accessed November 19, 2023.

- Zimmerman, Rachel. "How does trauma spill from one generation to the next?" *The Washington Post.* June 12, 2023. washingtonpost.com/wellness/2023/06/12/generational-trauma-passed-healing. Accessed November 19, 2023.

ACKNOWLEDGMENTS

TO ALL THE CHILDREN that I have had the honor of teaching; to the children all across the globe who have lost their peers and their teachers; to the students that I have taught and whose lives have been tragically cut short by gun violence—Tyson, Eric, Danny, Todd, and Omar; to Kip, whose death propelled me to run for elected office; and to the children still here creating waves and charting their own paths: know that you'll always have a place in my heart, and I will be right here to love and support you.

To my forward-thinking father, Eric, for his love and dedication to our family, and who passed away suddenly only a month after he worked the shirt off his back chopping wood so that I could attend teachers' college. To my beautiful and devoted mother, Mavis, who delivered me all by herself. I miss you dear confidante, advisor, and friend. To my beautiful, smart, and talented sister, Val, my friend, a dynamic teacher with a heart of gold, gone too soon—I will hold you forever in my heart and continue to fight and advocate for your Stars with steel determination. To my siblings, thank you for all of your love and undying support. We've been through so much together; thank you all for your faith, love, and prayers.

To my former teachers, Paula Edwards, Juliet Simpson, Paulette Forbes, Winston Phillips, and Thomas Aldridge, who took me under their wings, cared for me, loved me, supported me, know that I will do for kids what you did for me.

To all the little old ladies in my neighborhood who sent me to the shop and let me keep the change, thank you. To my mentors at Social Development Commission, many of whom are no longer here, know that your love and legacy lives on in the fight for justice.

And, of course, to Van Vassell, my darling husband, my rock, my comforter, and most ardent supporter, this book would not have been possible without your love and support. To my daughter, Alethe, and her husband, Jonathan; to my sons, Van Jr., Eric, and Terrence; and to my grandsons, Joseph and Elias. I love you all with every fiber of my being. This book wouldn't have been possible without every single one of you cheering me on! To my son, Terrence, for designing this beautiful book cover, thank you so much. To my siblings, students, friends, colleagues, neighbors, teachers, and social media supporters, some of whom I haven't met personally, thank you.

To my publisher, World Changers Media, and to Bryna Haynes, thank you for investing in this body of work. A big thank you to my editors and my book coach, Audra Figgins, for the countless hours spent coaching, proofing, and editing this treasure which will undoubtedly help to transform schools.

A huge thank you to all of the respondents who took the time and effort to participate in the survey to engage in candid interviews. Your offerings have been invaluable and have provided fuel for this book, which I know will be meaningful to educators and school leaders far and wide. To Frederick "Fred" the therapy dog at Central High, for your love and support of everyone in the building.

And finally, to my beloved hometown of Eleven Miles, Bull Bay, the community that cradled and protected me, I owe you a debt of gratitude. To the folks who didn't believe in me, didn't believe that I could rise above poverty and trauma to find peace and continued healing: thank you for lighting a fire of determination under me. Finally, to my Lord and Savior who has brought me this far, know that I will always be a conduit of your love and care.

ABOUT THE AUTHOR

MARCIA RANGLIN-VASSELL has not only survived the trauma of poverty and gun violence but she has also emerged as a beacon of hope, empathy, love, advocacy, and resilience. Her fight for justice and call to service began at the age of fourteen when she demonstrated for basic necessities such as water in her hometown. Undeterred by challenges, and with the support of her mentors at the Social Development Commission in Kingston, Jamaica, she extended her efforts to some of the most dangerous parts of East Kingston and Port Royal, initiating health education and youth programs.

Despite the many obstacles that Marcia faced after emigrating to the US, she persisted. Her motto is "I have no obstacles in my life; I turn all of them into stepping stones."

Steeped in faith while honoring her late parents, who set the stage for bold, compassionate public service, she continues the onward march to justice. Central to Marcia's philosophy and ideology is the conviction that those who escape the chokehold of poverty have a responsibility to extend a helping hand to others in need.

Marcia's emergence into politics in 2016 shook the landscape in Rhode Island when she challenged the House Majority Leader, a twenty-four-year incumbent she believed hadn't served the people of her district. Winning by a few votes in a primary election, her victory was described by political commentators as "an earthquake" and provided the template for future progressive candidates. Marcia's victory also ushered in a new era in Rhode Island, which saw Black, brown, and other marginalized groups of people running and winning elections. Her passionate and bold leadership shone a light on deep poverty in the state, as well as the plight of children.

Her own traumatic experience delivering twins set her on the path to exploring Black Maternal Mortality rates in a fellowship program on Maternal and Child Health with the National Conference of State Legislators (NCSL). Marcia's work in this area has been recognized and featured in the *Boston Globe*—"Here's what doulas do, and how they're fighting for Black maternal health"—as well as a PBS maternal health series, *The Risk of Giving Birth*. Fighting with advocates, allies, disruptors, and supporters, Marcia's work is continuing to transform maternal health for all women in Rhode Island, particularly Black and brown women. Because of her intentional work, Rhode Island has a model law for the country whereby private insurance companies now reimburse for doula services.

Her bold and public stance to end gun violence in the state gained attention from Moms Demand Action founder Shannon Watts. The issue gained local momentum and lit a strong fire with advocates and other legislators joining the public movement for good commonsense gun safety laws.

After three terms in the Rhode Island legislature, Marcia decided to prioritize her own physical and mental health by removing herself from the often toxic and traumatic arena of representational politics. Since then, she has given birth to her non-profit organization, Global Fund to End Childhood Hunger and Poverty. Marcia is not one to close doors and may, one day decide to run for public office again.

Marcia has earned several notable awards from organizations who have seen her and appreciate her resolute fight for the poor. Decades later, she continues her inspirational journey as a highly qualified public school teacher, inspiring both in and outside of the classroom. She considers herself a missionary doing God's work by attending to the needs of the poor, especially children.

Marcia is a graduate of St. Joseph's Teachers College, where she earned an Elementary Education diploma. She earned a Bachelor of Arts degree from Rhode Island College in Community Health Education, and a Master of Arts in Special Education from Providence College, as well as a Grades 7–12 Certification in English Language Arts. She's the author of *Journeys*, a collection of poems.

A born-again Christian, Marcia is a motivational speaker, trauma-informed presenter, advocate, and realistic poet. She's married to Van Vassell and has four adult children, Alethe, Van Jr., Eric, and Terrence, and two delightful grandsons, Joseph and Elias.

ABOUT THE PUBLISHER

FOUNDED IN 2021 by Bryna Haynes, WorldChangers Media is a boutique publishing company focused on "Ideas for Impact." We know that great books change lives, topple outdated paradigms, and build movements. Our commitment is to deliver superior-quality transformational nonfiction by, and for, the next generation of thought leaders.

Ready to write and publish your thought leadership book? Learn more at www.WorldChangers.Media.